GOD FOR GROWN-UPS

Discovering Christ today in the Catholic Church

A REDEMPTORIST PUBLICATION

Published by
Redemptorist Publications
Alphonsus House Chawton Alton Hampshire GU34 3HQ England

TEXT: Fr Kenneth O'Riordan
        Fr Gerry Murphy
        Sister Ellen McGrath

Originally published for Diocese of Nottingham by:
        Highfields Centre, Broadway, Derby

Design: Roger Smith
Editing: John Trenchard, C.SS.R.
Photographs: Cover: Zefa
            Hassocks from Church of St Andrew, Much Hadham, Hertfordshire

Extracts from "How to survive being married to a Catholic"
by Michael Henesy, C.SS.R. © Redemptorist Publications

Copyright © The Congregation of the Most Holy Redeemer

First Printing July 1995

Extract from 'The Face of Christ' by Daniel Berrigan

Extract from 'Canticle of the Sun'
Translation by Ezra Pound

ISBN 0 85231 152 4

Printed by:
Bourne Press Limited
Bournemouth, BH1 4QA

God for Grown-Ups
is a resource book for everyone
engaged in teaching the Catholic Faith
to adults. The starting point
for such teaching is the life and experience
of the inquirer. This experience
is then related to the experience
of Jesus Christ
and the Church.

God for Grown-Ups
is an essential aid for everyone
helping inquirers in the
Rite of Christian Initiation of Adults.
It explains the basic thinking
behind the R.C.I.A. process and offers
important background information
to the Rite based on practical experience.
God for Grown-Ups
suggests possible outlines for sessions
which help the catechist to take
those interested in the Catholic Faith
through from first inquiry
to the sacraments of initiation
and beyond.

CONTENTS

A INQUIRY PERIOD
(Period of Evangelisation)

B FORMATION PERIOD
(Period of Catechumenate)

C LENTEN PERIOD
(Period of Purification & Enlightenment)

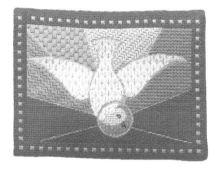

D EASTER PERIOD
(Period of Post-baptismal Catechesis or Mystagogy)

RCIA BASICS

The following notes are offered as background to the Rite of Christian Initiation of Adults. They help to clarify the 'thinking' and theology behind the Rite and outline some pastoral practicalities for those involved in leading the RCIA process. These notes should be read in conjunction with the Rite of Christian Initiation of Adults (published in English edition by Geoffrey Chapman, 1987).

The four periods or stages of R.C.I.A.

Sometimes it is thought that the periods of inquiry, formation, enlightenment and mystagogia are four consecutive steps. We can picture it like this:

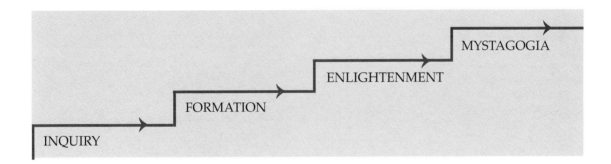

   With such a picture it is clearly impossible to do 'enlightenment' during the 'inquiry' period and vica versa.

   It might be more helpful to see that the four stages are part and parcel of the whole Church's life. They are the permanent dimensions of the whole parish's life.

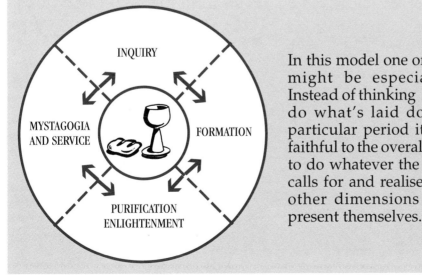

In this model one or all of the stages might be especially prevalent. Instead of thinking that one can only do what's laid down at any one particular period it might be more faithful to the overall life of the parish to do whatever the present moment calls for and realise that in time the other dimensions will inevitably present themselves.

What is the content?

"The Inquiry Period is a time of evangelisation: in faith and constancy the Living God is proclaimed, as in Jesus Christ, whom he sent for the salvation of all. Those who are not yet Christians, their hearts opened by the Holy Spirit, may believe and be freely converted to the Lord." *(R.C.I.A. Par 36)*

James Dunning complains that telling the Good News (evangelisation) is only half the story and regrets the Rite's omission of the need to listen to peoples' life stories. He warns that normally there is too much telling and lecturing and not enough listening to what inquirers feel the need for. Someone else wittily remarked that our concern has been to get Jones to swallow things rather than ask what would nourish him! What is at issue here is our assumptions and pictures of "faith". We have notionally moved away from seeing faith as "the acceptance of divinely revealed truths" and towards seeing it as "the entrusting of our whole selves freely to God offering the full submission of our mind and will". *(Vatican II Dogmatic Constitution on Divine Revelation 5)* In practice, however, there is too much of "the parish R.C.I.A. team instructs Jones". We bring other assumptions about who 'has' faith and who 'hasn't'! In the Rite there is an assumption that *God has already been present in this inquirer's life*. Our task is more to help them personally spot God's presence and absence.

No one comes to R.C.I.A. without some kind of "faith". It's not that they previously lacked faith and are now searching for it but rather that they have come to distrust the faith by which they have been living and are now seeking to discover what it would be like to live by faith revealed in the life and death of Jesus. So our task becomes one of helping them to be aware of the faith they have been living by *so that* they can contrast it with gospel faith. One of the best ways of doing this is to emphasise the importance of "Knowing the Time" *(John 4:20f)* of our lives. We need to ask first of all "what time is it for this person, this group, this parish?" This might help us catch the raw nerve and truly respond to the action of God in the inquirer's life *now*. Otherwise, we tyrannise inquirers and ourselves by our preoccupation with content and programmes which might be full of other peoples' questions and concerns but are not those of these inquirers.

Four means of formation

Growth in the Christian life is achieved in four ways and these four ways are indicated in the Introdution to the Rite.

1. Dogma

"A *fitting* formation accommodated to the liturgical year and enriched by celebrations of the word leads the catechumens to a *suitable knowledge* of dogma and also an *intimate understanding* of the mystery of salvation." *(R.C.I.A. Par.75. 1)*

The key words here are underlined *fitting, suitable, intimate.* They all speak of personal knowledge, heart knowledge, something that becomes part of "me". To know what's suitable it is necessary *to know the time in this person's life.* They should be helped to read "the signs of the times" in their lives:

- children growing up,
- someone dying,
- a dissatisfaction,
- nuclear threat etc..

Intimacy cannot be programmed – it happens when the time is right. It also happens because the right word is said at the right time. Dogma becomes whatever in the Gospel is Good News to these particular people now.

2. Morality

> "Familiar with living the Christian way of life and helped by the example and support of sponsors and godparents and the whole community of the faithful the catechumens will learn to pray to God more easily and exercise charity towards neighbours to the point of self-renunciation." *(R.C.I.A. Par.75.2)*

There is the closest connection between what we believe and how we live. We don't first know Jesus and then follow him. Like the disciples we come to know him *by* following him. It is the experience of trying to live the Christian way which throws up discoveries, challenges, questions. We need to find out what is happening to the inquirers *in their attempts at living the gospel.*

3. Prayer and Liturgy

The secret is knowing when and how to celebrate. Prayer is not tacked on to sessions. Instead it should express the "deep story" of what's happening to all of us: it points to something we can't find words for.

We don't pray because we already understand or are already fully committed. Rather, we submit ourselves to prayer and the rites in order to discover something, something about living by faith.

As the Rite says this happens "little by little" *(R.C.I.A. Par.75.3)*. It could add "painfully" too.

4. Apostolate

> "Since the Church's life is apostolic, catechumens should also learn how to work actively with others to spread the gospel and build up the Church by the testimony of their lives and the profession of their faith." *(R.C.I.A. Par.75.4)*

This is not "bible bashing" or spreading propaganda as Pope Paul VI made clear in *Evangelii Nuntiandi*, but it means living in such a way as to attract others and raise questions in their minds. It is also about responding to the seeking of others; knowing when it's time to speak and when it's time to keep silence.

These four elements are taken from the guidelines for the catechumenate period but their spirit obviously also informs the inquiry period. They clearly show us how the Rite officially encourages us to break away from our preoccupations with content and set programmes and become more responsive to the call of God in the *present* of these inquirers' lives.

Teaching and learning methods in R.C.I.A.

The above "four means of formation" describe the methods of conversion in R.C.I.A.

- suitable knowledge of dogma,
- Christian living,
- prayer and liturgy,
- reaching out to others.

There is a tendency to emphasize the dogma at the expense of the other three influences. Perhaps this is because we look at most of our life through a *"rear-view mirror"* and we remain chained to the patterns of the past. We teach others as we have been taught ourselves. We form others as we have been formed.

The truth is that **"LIFE EXPERIENCE** – our own, that of other people, especially that of Jesus, **IS THE CONTENT OF THE GOSPEL"**.

In other words, "instruction" is not enough. The RCIA team is not there to do the "instruction" previously done by the priest. The "lecture" method of delivering prepared talks becomes wholly inadequate when we believe consistently in a grassroots God, enfleshed, incarnate, the beyond in our midst. With such faith we aim to put others in touch with a God already acting in their lives and especially in the life of Jesus.

So we begin with a "bottom-up" rather than a "top-down" model of God and Church. As J Dunning says:

"Through dialogue between inquirers and Jesus, between their lives and his life, catechists do not bring God to where God wasn't. Rather they help people discover a presence that has always been. You can't lecture a discovery. You can give information, the only justified purpose of lecture, which allows transformation and celebration." *(Ministries: Sharing God's Gifts, page 87)*

Monological v Dialogical lecture

A monological lecture talks *at* people, giving answers to questions they themselves have not raised. A dialogical lecture talks *with* people, even though they say nothing out loud. A dialogical lecturer has listened to the lives of people and the Life of Jesus and makes connections. When that happens we say it "rings bells", "makes me think", "me too", and the conversation and change continues within ourselves.

A Praxis method of education

This is a way of actually doing much of what has been recommended above. It is the method which permeates this book.

PRAXIS means reflection in the midst of action, noticing the signs, the responses of people, listening to the vibes. John Shea calls it "thinking on the battlefield". It seeks to avoid applying theory to practice and instead reflects *in* the doing, the living.

This praxis method is taken from "Christian Religious Education" by Tom Groome, especially chapters 9 and 10. It has five independent movements. You can start logically with the first movement but also it's possible to start with the third and then complete the circle.

1. Your present concern and story
2. Reflecting on your story
3. The Christian story and Vision
4. Letting the two stories speak to each other
5. New behaviour

Movement one: *Your present action*

What is your story, your past and present experience about the issue in hand, e.g. suffering?

Movement two: *The why question*

Asking deeper questions of your experience and action. Uncovering our underlying assumptions about the issue, e.g. why care for my ageing parents?

Movement three: *The Christian community story and vision*

What does the Christian Community have to say about this issue - the Bible Story, the tradition and practice of the Church?

Movement four: *Dialogue between my experience and the Christian community experience*

How does the Christian story add to your story? Does your story add anything to the Christian story? Where do you agree/disagree? What seems wisdom and nonsense to you?

Movement five: *New action*

How does this reflection make you want to change, alter, deepen your living in this area? The Word became not theory but flesh!

Each movement is important and shouldn't be omitted. The second and the fourth are especially difficult and crucial. No method can march a person to conversion. Really the key test for any educational method is the *respect* it pays to the unique journey of each inquirer and the *challenge* it poses towards new living.

Pre-inquiry period interview

Before the group meets it is important to meet each inquirer individually to find out a little about what's attracting him or her to the Catholic Church. The leader also needs to be aware of such other relevant information as:

- present religion, baptism,
- marriage/remarriage details,
- family situation, job, Catholic friends,
- present questions about becoming a Catholic, expectations and fears about this group, etc.

Such information as is gained would need to be shared confidentially between priests and catechists who would then begin to sense how to "tailor" the programme to suit the needs of these inquirers.

Who are the inquirers?

All types! People who are in some way dissatisfied with their lives and want something "more". Some have been coming to Mass for thirty years and had never been asked. Others have a Catholic husband or wife. Some have met the parish through the baptism, communion, confirmation preparation of their children. Others through sickness and death. Some go to the Social Club and Parish Dances. Some have met Catholics at work or next door. Others have been touched by Pope John Paul's stand on "justice".

We need to actively reach out to all these people and not just wait for them to come to us. We do so in the spirit of freedom and respect, assuring them that this is an *offer, not propaganda or indoctrination.* We need to create the right spirit so that they feel free to come but also leave. In general a *no strings attached approach* seems to be best: a basic commitment to take part for two or three months and then a decision to continue or withdraw.

How to reach them

Personal contact and personal invitation works best: also newsletters, sermons, press advertisements and word of mouth. Somehow the whole parish community needs to reach out.

Who are the ministers?

"The Initiation of Catechumens takes place step by step *in the midst of the community of the faithful.*" (R.C.I.A. Par.4)

It is the whole community of the parish which is called to minister and not just an "elite" on the R.C.I.A. team.

Before inquirers present themselves publicly they have probably had informal ministers for some years – a married partner, a friend or neighbour. These people have already "ministered" to the inquirers and their particular ministry needs to be acknowledged, celebrated and deepened. Also there are in each parish those who would never dream of being on the R.C.I.A. team but who are "interested" in people and have a special feel for newcomers. They know how to welcome, to make inquirers feel they belong and are wanted, they invite them to their houses spontaneously and "chat" without inhibition. This group of informal welcomers needs to be highlighted and put in the picture.

Those who befriend and welcome need to see that they don't *just* make the tea!

Selecting and training an R.C.I.A. core team – catechists and sponsors as we call them

It is important to recognise that everyone can't be a catechist or sponsor. It is a particular gift, a talent that can be developed and improved. So catechists and sponsors have to be chosen with care and not just accepted because there's nobody else who's volunteered. Some hints for selecting catechists could be:-

1. People who have raised their own questions, who know their own stories, who haven't got it altogether but who have dared to "journey" and grow in their faith.

2. People who are open to the continuing conversion process in their own lives.

3. People who are willing and able to share their own stories with others.

4. People who know the key stories of the scriptures, who have been exposed to Catholic practices and who know where to look to find answers to ordinary questions.

5. People who are great listeners – who make others feel that they can "talk to them" about anything that's on their minds. People who can embrace the shy, the talkative, and even those obsessed with Catholic minutiae.

6. People who know that learning and conversation often doesn't happen during the group session but rather on the way home in the car or over a cup of coffee in the week.

Such people will form a team comprised of a variety of men and women, of ages, of classes, of spiritualities.

Training

Full training is impossible: nor is it desirable. If the right kind of team has been selected they will learn "on the job". Clearly, it is helpful if the team can include people who have already experienced the RCIA process.

In most dioceses help will be available from trained catechists or from area support groups.

Sponsors

Each inquirer needs a sponsor. Sometimes this is a married partner or Catholic friend. Otherwise the parish community should select people who would be interested and suitable. It is unwise to try to match inquirers with permanent sponsors in the first few sessions: it is better to let things evolve, watching who best gets on with who. You'll probably find after a while that the inquirer will suggest who he or she would like for her particular sponsor.

There should be one or two *training sessions for sponsors* before the group begins so that expectations are clear – this could focus on the spirit of the whole conversion process and the role of the sponsor as companion, guide and witness.

It is desirable for the sponsors to meet together at each stage of the initiation process to give feedback on their candidates and to familiarise themselves with the particular stage or period.

Learning to work as a team

This is probably one of biggest sources of tension in the RCIA process. We are all so different! Different personalities, different ways of working, different theologies and spiritualities, different ways of planning and preparing. Needless to say the relationships between the teams reflect to the inquirers what the Church is really like. Maybe we should expect more seriously that the team members have to journey together – this involves finding out about each other, listening, sharing, challenging, honesty, care, patience, forgiveness and realising that no one of us has it all: we genuinely need each other because of the differences! Regular team meetings are important. Sometimes what most needs talking out are the feelings of team members towards each other, especially the role and person of the priest.

How long should it take?

One of the dangers with some current RCIA practice – September to May – is that it could "steamroller" some inquirers. We need to be clear that the RCIA process is for these particular people and not the other way round. It might be that some people need a longer inquiry or formation period. The Rite itself says that the formation period "may last for several years". (R.C.I.A. Par.7) Everything depends "on the grace of God, the cooperation of individual inquirers and the help of the local community". (R.C.I.A. Par.76)

The Rite says "nothing can be determined a priori, about how long it takes" (R.C.I.A. Par. 76). We are called to be respectful to the particular faith of each inquirer – it may be that they stop coming to the group but remain in touch informally. It is also possible to continue in the group without becoming a catechumen. The Rite emphasises flexibility – it can take several years.

Leading and running the group

Each person – including catechists and sponsors– will probably come to the group with certain gut fears:

- will they like me?
- will they hurt me?
- will I succeed here?

It is the task of catechists and sponsors to create an atmosphere where every one begins to feel at home – where people feel respected, trusted and safe.

Organise small groups of 3 or 4. If possible, vary the groups and put a catechist or sponsor in each group.

Some do's

- Learn everyone's name at the first session and use their Christian name when you talk to them.
- Introduce people to each other.
- Remember groups begin slowly and nervously.

SUGGESTED READING TO ACCOMPANY GOD FOR GROWN-UPS

Rite of Christian Initiation of Adults, *Definitive Edition*

Catechism of the Catholic Church, *(The Vatican)*

Documents of Vatican II

Your Faith *(Redemptorist Publications)*

Guide to Sponsors: R Lewinski, *(McCrimmon)*

How to form a Catechumenate Team: K Hinman, *(McCrimmon)*

The Book of Sacramental Basis: T Guzie, *(Paulist)*

Guidelines: Living and Sharing Our Faith: Jim Gallagher, *(Collins)*

Stories of Faith: John Shea, *(Fowler Wright)*

Stories of God: John Shea, *(Fowler Wright)*

Storytelling – Imagination and Faith: W Bausch, *(Columba)*

*"This is a time of evangelisation...
so that those who are
not yet Christians, their hearts opened
by the Holy Spirit,
may believe and be freely
converted to the Lord and
commit themselves sincerely to him.
For he who is the way, the truth,
and the life fulfils all
their spiritual expectations,
indeed infinitely surpasses them."*

(Rite)

The Good Shepherd

THE INQUIRY PERIOD

(Period of Evangelisation)

Prayer and liturgy in the inquiry period

The Rite of becoming Catechumens is the formal liturgy for this period. It is normally celebrated on the first Sunday of Advent at Mass and it presumes the inquirers "have accepted the first proclamation of the Living God and already have an elementary faith in Christ the Saviour". *(R.C.I.A. Par.41 ff)* There's a sense in which this Rite marks not one but three beginnings.

1. It is a beginning in faith

It recognises that the conversion process has already begun. The seeds are beginning to grow. The candidates are given the name "Christian". They become members of the Church *now* and *not* in the Rite of Baptism.

2. It is the beginning of Liturgical Life

Until now there have been no formal liturgical celebrations because we cannot presume the necessary faith. In this initial conversion to Christ and the Church the candidates become part of the believing community.

3. It is the inquirers' initial formal contact with the worshipping community

They are formally presented to all the people at Mass. They are welcomed and prayed for by those they don't know.

The Parish Community

The parish community needs to be put and *kept* in the picture at all the different stages of the journey.

i.   when inviting inquirers at the very beginning
ii. when the group of inquirers begins to meet
iii. immediately before the Rite of Acceptance into the Order of Catechumens.

This could be done by preaching, by bidding prayers, through the newsletter, and informally. Often our parish communities are not adequately informed and prepared for what is going to happen. A leaflet for this Rite, distributed to all the congregation, might be helpful. A social gathering afterwards might prove a more informal welcome.

Before the Rite interview

This seems to be necessary at least three weeks beforehand to find out whether the inquirer feels ready to formally continue on the journey towards (full) initiation. This interview is probably best done by priest and catechists and indeed "it is the responsibility of pastors to judge the external indications of the inquirers dispositions". *(R.C.I.A. Par.43)*

The criteria recommended in the Rite for Acceptance into the Order of Catechumens include:
1) initial conversion and desire to change one's life
2) the desire to enter into contact with God in Christ
3) first sense of repentance
4) the practice of calling on God and praying
5) the first experience of the society and spirit of Christians. *(R.C.I.A. Par.42)*

Distinguishing between the already Baptised and Unbaptised inquirers

Frequently, there is insufficient awareness of the importance and necessity of this distinction. There is a growing consciousness of, and sensitivity to, the baptismal status of those who are part of other Christian Churches. We need to ensure that for those who enter the process of conversion both the baptised and unbaptised embark on similar journeys of the heart. What can be tricky is the *liturgical sensitivity* that a parish must use in *the celebration of the rituals* that mark the stages of conversion and the thresholds from one period to another. A pastoral solution finds a parish celebrating the rite with both groups – the baptised and the unbaptised – at the same celebration, carefully wedding the two groups in a common liturgical experience. This is done in such a way as to keep the two groups distinguished by *differences in language* (of the prayers) and *in seating arrangement.* As long as respect is given to *both* groups and to the commitment of those already baptised this is a possible option. It is not a question of separating catechumens and the already baptised like sheep and goats but rather of planting and watering different seeds so that all might flower in due season.

The dismissal

During and after the Rite of Becoming Catechumens it is recommended that the catechumens are "dismissed" after the Liturgy of the Word and before the Eucharist.

"Ordinarily, when they are present in the assembly of the faithful they should be kindly dismissed before the liturgy of the eucharist begins (unless their dismissal would present practical or pastoral problems)." *(R.C.I.A. Par 75;3)*

The Rite gives a prayer formula for dismissal *(Par.67)* and says "the group of catechumens goes out but does not disperse. With the help of some of the faithful they remain to share their joy and spiritual experiences".

It is still relatively unusual for parishes to "dismiss" the catechumens. Obviously it calls for more commitment on the part of the priest and RCIA team: they have to pray and share with the catechumens afterwards; they have to carefully explain the Rite to both the catechumens and parish community so that both see why the dismissal is happening and don't see it as rejection; they also have to see the need for *gradualism* – the catechumens are still beginning and growing and can be best helped when things are presented in small pieces and then broken down. In short, it is easy to see why parishes don't commonly celebrate the Dismissal – it is very demanding! One of the results that should not be underestimated, however, is its effect on the Catholics who remain for the Eucharist who are encouraged to think again about what it is they are celebrating and what commitment is called for on their part.

The structure of each session

This applies to each evening except the introductory sessions:

STEP 1:	My Story – involving exercises	10 minutes
	– personal stories	40 minutes
STEP 2:	Scripture Story	30 minutes
STEP 3:	How the stories touch each other	15 minutes
STEP 4:	Liturgy	15 minutes
STEP 5:	To talk over with your sponsor	During the week
TEA	Possibly after Step 1	10 minutes

Alternative Routes
for the Inquiry Period

The suggested themes outlined in these Sessions are not intended to be comprehensive; nor is it possible to suggest themes that would include all aspects of the Christian life. There are many areas to be explored and these **"alternative routes"** are proposed, with some possible reading material, to remind readers of other significant themes and to help in the process of discovering the treasures of our Faith.

This Parish's Story
People are the main resource – old and middle-aged and young people. And don't forget the parish newsletters, newspaper clippings, anniversary booklets, registers, photographs, etc.

The Universal Search for Meaning
Help my Unbelief:
Michael Paul Gallagher, *(Veritas)*
When bad things happen to good people:
Harold Kushner, *(Pan)*
Catechism of the Catholic Church

The Bible and my Life
**God Speaks to You:
The Old Testament,**
(Harper Collins)
**God Speaks to You:
The New Testament,**
(Harper Collins)
The Bible Makes Sense:
Walter Brueggemann, *(SCM)*
How to Read the Old Testament:
E Charpentier, *(SCM)*
**How to Read the
New Testament:**
E Charpentier, *(SCM)*

Immediate Church Questions
Your Faith: a popular presentation of Catholic belief, *(Redemptorist Publications)*
We Believe: an introduction to the belief of Catholics today, *(CTS)*
We Live: an introduction to the practice of Catholicism today, *(CTS)*
How to survive being married to a Catholic:
(Redemptorist Publications)
The Catholic Faith:
R Strange, *(Oxford)*

Introductory evening
General background

R.C.I.A. is fundamentally a story telling process: our own personal stories, each others stories, the Church's stories.

Something happens when we tell the stories of our own lives and listen to those of others. Our hearts and lives are touched, illuminated and changed. The person telling gets so involved that they merge with the tale. The hearer moves from being an observer to becoming a participant. This is what makes stories interesting. They touch us all in a primitive, more than rational way.

Stories are also accessible to everyone. Many people feel out of their depth with an intellectual or theoretical approach. But everyone tells stories and listens to them. To ask someone what they really believe about life is often to be greeted by an embarrassed silence. Ask them to tell of a time when they felt "up against it" is to reach the question of "beliefs" through the world of story. The mystery of story is that everyone is one and has some – in a conducive setting everyone wants to tell one.

Stories are not the practical examples of abstract ideas. Rather they are the rawest expression and ordering of the tumult of human experience. They do not simply illustrate the ideas of the mind: they come *before* that and give rise to ideas as fire gives rise to smoke. Any story is open to many interpretations – when it's told to different people it generates different understandings. *This needs to be welcomed and accepted. There is never only one right meaning – the process is much richer than that.*

The Story is able to meet us where we are without forcing us into where we should be. We're allowed to draw what *we need* from the story but we are also provoked into fresh insight and action.

Running this session

Listen carefully, really carefully, to *what* the inquirers say tonight and also to *how* they say it. Remember that whatever they say is like the tip of an iceberg concealing more than it reveals. Expect shyness, caution, reluctance and fear. Encourage them to say as much or as little as they want. Be ready to share a little of your story of wanting to be involved in this process with them – what is it that attracts you this year?

Give name tags to everyone. In the introduction ask people to speak to someone they don't know very well and then tell the whole group about them. In "Why I am here" tell them these are not trick questions and there are no right answers. Value whatever they say in response. In "What we're offering" outline the months ahead and the four stages or steps in the journey. Stress that at the end of each step the inquirer will be asked whether they want to proceed – there will be no arm-twisting. Talk about the inquiry period between now and Christmas – in the next two sessions they will be helped to feel comfortable in the church building. In the following nine sessions we will emphasize what's underneath and sometimes hidden behind our religious practices – how we meet God in daily living. Explain

1

that you want to tailor the programme to their needs and so would welcome feedback each week and at the end of this period.

Summary of inquiry period

INTRODUCTION	IN THE CHURCH	GOD IN DAILY LIVING
1	2 3	4 5 6 7 8 9 10 11 12

RITE OF BECOMING CATECHUMENS	EVALUATION AND LOOKING TO THE FUTURE
13	14

Take some care over the liturgies – don't miss them out because of running late! For each session find a small table, cloth, candle, some flowers and music.

1. Introduction

Names (tags), where you live, who's in your family.

2. Catechists, sponsors and priest

Say what their role is to the group, i.e. welcomer, teacher, friend, companion, supporter on the journey into the Catholic Community.

3. Why am I here?

Agree/Disagree (Mark tick or cross or question mark in each box)

	I'm here because I've decided to become a Catholic.
	I'm here because I'm curious about the Catholic Church.
	I'm here because my friend invited me and they impressed me.
	I'm here because I'm not happy with my own Church.
	I'm here because my wife/husband's a Catholic and I feel a bit left out.
	I'm here because I'm marrying a Catholic.
	I'm here because something has happened in my life that's made me think.
	I'm here because I want to help the children more.
	I'm here because Father asked me to help.
	I'm here because although I'm already a Catholic I want to learn more about it.
	_____?

Share your responses with the person next to you and then in the larger group.

(Copy of this questionnaire for photocopying on page 24)

4. *What are we offering*

Explanation by the whole team of the programme between now and Pentecost.

5. *Small groups and large groups*

For reactions, clarifications guided by catechist or sponsor.

6. *Liturgy*

Light a candle and play some music to create a quiet, peaceful atmosphere.

Let us Pray

God our Father, we ask you to help us become aware of your presence in the world, found in many people and in the various circumstances they encounter. Help each one of us to gain deeper insights into our faith, that together we may be able to discover your values, to know what to do and how to do it. We make this prayer through your Son, Jesus Christ our Lord.

All: Amen.

Reading: Ephesians 1: 3-14

Choose a suitable hymn for this evening e.g.,
         Firmly I believe.
         Walk with me O my Lord.
         You shall cross the barren desert.

Let us offer each other a sign of peace.

Blessing: May the Lord bless us and give us the courage to open our hearts and minds to his love.

All: Amen.

Why am I here?

Agree/Disagree (Mark tick or cross or question mark in each box)

☐ I'm here because I've decided to become a Catholic.

☐ I'm here because I'm curious about the Catholic Church.

☐ I'm here because my friend invited me and they mpressed me.

☐ I'm here because I'm not happy with my own Church.

☐ I'm here because my wife/husband's a Catholic and I feel a bit left out.

☐ I'm here because I'm marrying a Catholic.

☐ I'm here because something has happened in my life that's made me think.

☐ I'm here because I want to help the children more.

☐ I'm here because Father asked me to help.

☐ I'm here because although I'm already a Catholic I want to learn more about it.

☐ _____?

Share your responses with the person next to you and then in the larger group.

A tour around the Church

1. Most of the inquirers will already be going to Mass so they will be familiar with some of the following. We suggest that you literally walk people around the different parts of the church beginning at the door. There you could talk about who greets them, welcomes them, opens the door to them in your church. Point out the holy water fonts and ask one of them to show the group how to bless oneself. Ask them why we do this each time we enter and leave the church building

2. Proceed into the body of the church and seat all the group in the front benches. Show them how to genuflect and ask them why we do so upon entering and leaving the church. This leads to the Mass and the tabernacle and sanctuary lamp which tell of the reservation of the "Blessed Sacrament" from Mass. Be aware of each of them telling their story and encourage questions. It might be possible to open the tabernacle and show what's inside.

3. Point out the crucifix as one of the most important pictures we have of Jesus. Speak about the different types of crucifix – "traditional, the High Priest, Celtic, Jesus crowned, Coptic, Armenian, etc.

4. Briefly talk through the actions of the Mass: the gathering of the people together; the President's chair; the lectern and the telling of the Scripture stories; the preparation of the gifts and the eucharistic prayer at the altar; the breaking of bread and communion; the dismissal and going home. Emphasize that all this is *an introduction* to topics you will address in detail later.

5. It would be fitting to finish the session by praying together in the church. Perhaps a hymn, a Scripture reading from the lectern and the 'Our Father'.

3 In the Church – special Catholic practices

Again assemble at the front of the church, recap upon the previous session, invite any comments or questions and then introduce this sesion – "The Different Ways Catholics Pray."

1. Start with the Stations of the Cross. Take people around the church, looking at each one and telling its story. You might like to pray together at one or two nearer the end.

2. Take people to the Lady Chapel. Talk about the special honour we give to Mary, the mother of Jesus and mother of the Church. Talk about the importance and dignity of women, motherhood, the poor and humble and "the feminine" in God and in each one of us. This could be done by talking about the words of the "Hail Mary". You might like to light a candle and sing a hymn.

3. Who is the patron saint of your parish? To which mystery of Faith is your parish dedicated? How are the qualities of this saint or this mystery expressed in the life of your parish?

4. Often there are other statues in the church – of the Sacred Heart, St. Joseph, St. Martin, etc. These remind us of how we are part of a Church which lives both in heaven and on earth – the people of the past intercede for us and lead us into the future.

5. Many people will be curious and a bit afraid of the confessional or "reconciliation room". You might like to take them into it; show them what we do; tell them you will look at the question in detail after Christmas.

4-7
Introduction to immediate questions about Catholics

These next four sessions
deal with immediate questions
about the Catholic Church.
The issues – Catholics and the Mass,
Catholics and the Pope, Catholics and Confession,
Catholics and Mary – relate to the issues
most frequently raised by inquirers.
These sessions are intended to open questions
and so the coverage is not complete.
They should all be revisited during the
catechumenate period.

You might find that your inquirers
have different or other questions about Catholics.
Find out what they are and respond to them.

It is intended that *the method* used below is
applicable to whatever issue is chosen.

4

Catholics and the Mass
Step one: My Story

Recap the previous session and deal briefly with comments, observations and feedback.

Introduce the next block on 'What Catholics Believe and Live'. Mention the four topics chosen and say there is room for others of their own choice.

Introduce the format of these sections. It is based on the praxis method mentioned in RCIA BASICS on pages 10-11.

When introducing the 'My Story' section, emphasise that we are looking for what people themselves really think and feel and so there are no right and wrong answers. Ask them to tick whatever they want. In the feedback don't judge any of their answers – let them ride and point out the variety, richness and validity of each angle. Judgement will come in the third step, 'How the Stories Touch Each Other'.

Agree/Disagree with the following. (Mark tick, cross or question mark in each box)

For me, Mass means a time:

	in the week when I slow down and get things in perspective.
	when I worry about when to sit and kneel and make the sign of the cross.
	when I feel welcomed and befriended by the other people there.
	when I find the Bible stories hard to identify with.
	when I sometimes recognise myself in the Bible stories.
	when I find the singing picks me up and gives me new heart.
	when I feel left out at Communion time.
	when I feel united with others especially through the sign of peace.
	when I come away thinking about my life in a new way.
	when I come home feeling puzzled or untouched.

Going to Mass for me means ....

In pairs share your responses. A leader then records the groups' responses.

(Copy of the questionnaire for photocopying on page 32)

Reflecting on my story

A leader then invites the group to reflect upon their responses. Sometimes he or she might share their own reflections to enable the group to understand what is being asked. The leader might ask such questions as:

Who are the people
What are the events, experiences } **that have led you to give these**
What is the reading, media coverage } **responses?**

Again this can be discussed in pairs and then gathered together. A further question might then be:

What would your ideal experience of Mass be like?
What would be the best celebration of Mass for you?

Step two: the Catholic Community Story

A leader speaks for 5 – 10 minutes on the most pertinent elements of this story. The notes below are intended as *background* and not as a verbatim 'talk'.

The Bible and Tradition
The Passover meal

It's origins are described in detail in Exodus Chapter 12 and Chapter 13: 1-10. It is the meal the Jewish people eat each year when they remember how what happened to them in the past (a people enslaved in Egypt became free in the promised land) is mysteriously made present *now* in the lives of the participants. The old story is retold and the participants are invited to see how the very same thing is happening in a new way within their own lives and time.

The Last Supper

This reminds us of all the meals Jesus had eaten with people, especially with 'the tax collectors and sinners'. This last meal was celebrated with his apostles (another very mixed bunch) in the context of a passover meal. It involved the ritual actions of the passover meal with a completely new interpretation. Jesus took the Bread and the Cup and gave them a new meaning. From then on they are to be the living memory of *his* life, death and resurrection which *we* are to *do*.

The Last Supper involves all the elements of the Passover Meal, cf. Matthew 26:17-30.
1) The preparation.
2) Gathering together in a prepared place.
3) Re-telling the old story which now becomes the new story of Jesus.
4) The Blessing, breaking and giving of the Bread.
5) Taking the Cup, giving thanks, sharing the Cup.
6) Pointing to the future (Jesus' betrayal, death and resurrection).

4

Saint Paul

Paul is the earliest writer to record the story he was given about the Last Supper. He notes the context, the main elements, and finally the stark connection between celebrating the Eucharist and living (or not living) it.

'For this is what I received from the Lord, and in turn passed on to you: that on the same night that he was betrayed, the Lord Jesus took some bread, and thanked God for it and broke it, and he said, "This is my body, which is for you; do this as a memorial of me". In the same way he took the cup after supper, and said, "This cup is the new covenant in my blood. Whenever you drink it, do this as a memorial of me". Until the Lord comes, therefore, every time you eat this bread and drink this cup, you are proclaiming his death.' *(1 Corinthians 11:23-26)*

Early Christian communities

They called the Eucharist 'the breaking of bread' and included it as part of the essence of what it meant to follow Jesus in the contemporary world. Notice once again how celebrating the Eucharist expressed what they were living and wasn't some foreign thing merely tacked onto their lives.

Acts 2: 42-47 "These remained faithful to the teaching of the apostles, to the brotherhood, to the breaking of bread and to the prayers. The many miracles and signs worked through the apostles made a deep impression on everyone. The faithful all lived together and owned everything in common; they sold their goods and possessions and shared out the proceeds among themselves according to what each one needed. They went as a body to the Temple every day but met in their houses for the breaking of bread; they shared their food gladly and generously; they praised God and were looked up to by everyone. Day by day the Lord added to their community those destined to be saved."

Second Vatican Council 1962 -65

Vatican II reformed the celebration of the Eucharist within the Catholic Church. Point out some of the emphases and changes introduced. Consult 'The Constitution on the Liturgy' especially Chapter 2 *(The Documents of Vatican II).*

Exercises

After the input, small groups are formed to react.
Such questions as below might be helpful.

- **What was new?**
- **What was confirmed from the past?**
- **What was unclear?**
- **What do you not agree with?**
- **What do you want to know more about?**

The small groups should then feed back and their findings recorded.

Step three: How do our stories touch each other?

Looking at the two pieces of paper notice what's similar, what's different, and what light they shed on each other.

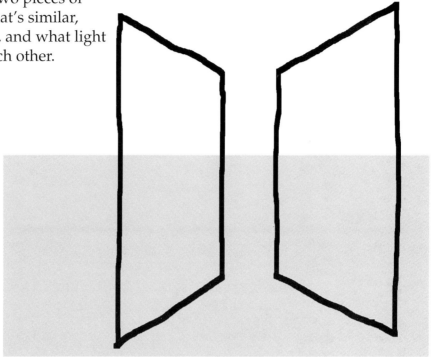

Step four: Prayer time

On a small table place a candle and some oil. Play some music to create a peaceful, quiet atmosphere. Light the candle.

- **Re-read one of the Bible Stories.**
- **Pray a prayer. Sing a hymn.**
- **Invite the group to consider how they feel called to change as a result of this discussion.**

Step five: To talk over with a Catholic friend or sponsor

- My reactions, my thoughts and feelings about this issue.
- What I like, dislike, don't understand, want to know more about.
- How I feel called to look at it from a new angle.

For me, Mass means a time...

Agree/Disagree with the following. (Mark tick, cross or question mark in each box)

☐ in the week when I slow down and get things in perspective.

☐ when I worry about when to sit and kneel and make the sign of the cross.

☐ when I feel welcomed and befriended by the other people there.

☐ when I find the Bible stories hard to identify with.

☐ when I sometimes recognise myself in the Bible stories.

☐ when I find the singing picks me up and gives me new heart.

☐ when I feel left out at Communion time.

☐ when I feel united with others especially through the sign of peace.

☐ when I come away thinking about my life in a new way.

☐ when I come home feeling puzzled or untouched.

Going to Mass for me means _____

_____

_____

In pairs share your responses.

Catholics and the Pope
Step one: *My Story*

Recap the previous session and deal briefly with comments and feedback.

Ask people to tick or cross the boxes as they like. Emphasise there are no right or wrong answers. Record their feedback without judging it.

Agree/Disagree with the following (Mark tick, cross or question mark in each box)

When I think of the Pope I think:

☐	of someone to give us strong leadership.
☐	I am anxious about him telling me how to live my life.
☐	we need one person to unite all the different peoples.
☐	of Pope John Paul II and like his personable approach.
☐	of Pope John Paul II and find him a bit like a superstar.
☐	of why he doesn't sell more of the Church's riches.
☐	of the doctrine of infallibility which I don't really understand.
☐	of something else which strikes me.

In pairs share your responses. A leader then records the groups' responses.

(Copy of this questionnaire for photocopying on page 37)

Reflecting on my story

A leader then invites the group to reflect upon their responses. Sometimes he or she might share their own reflections to enable the group to understand what is being asked. The leader might ask such questions as:

Who are the people
What are the events, experiences } **that have led you to give these**
What is the reading, media coverage } **responses?**

Again this can be discussed in pairs and then gathered together. A further question might then be:

What is your ideal Pope?
What is your dream of how a Pope should be?

5

Step two: The Catholic Community Story

A leader speaks for 5 – 10 minutes on the most pertinent elements of this story. The notes below are intended as *background* and not as a verbatim 'talk'.

The Bible and Tradition
Catholics and the Pope

a) Simon Peter is traditionally the first disciple called by Jesus to follow him. Cf. Mt. 4:18ff; Mark 1:16ff; Luke 5: 1-11. Peter is the fisherman who is to be a fisher of men. In John's Gospel Simon Peter is the first one to have the news "We have found the Messiah" announced to him by his brother Andrew. *(John 1: 35-42)* Also in John Chapter 1, Simon Peter is given the name "Cephas" meaning Rock by Jesus.

b) In all the Gospels it is Peter's name that heads the list of disciples and Apostles (those who are sent by Jesus). He is almost always the spokesperson for the group.

c) In John's Gospel the beloved disciple waits for Peter to enter the empty tomb and witness the binding cloths left behind by the Risen Lord.

d) He is the one who makes, on behalf of all the Apostles, the triple act of faith and love, "Yes Lord, you know that I love you" and is given the commission to "Feed my lambs", "Tend my sheep" and "Feed my sheep".

e) Peter is the one who in the synoptic tradition (Matthew, Mark, Luke) identifies Jesus as "the Christ, the Son of the Living God", and who, on behalf of the group, is the Rock on which the church, *ecclesia*, the gathering of God's people, will be built. The power of binding and unbinding given to Peter in Mt.16:18 is given to the whole community of disciples in Mt.18:15-20; and in John's tradition, to the whole group of disciples in the gift of the Holy Spirit to the Church: Cf. John 20:22ff "Receive the Holy Spirit. For those whose sins you forgive, they are forgiven; for those whose sins you retain, they are retained".

f) Simon Peter is traditionally the first Bishop-episkopos of Rome: Rome, the capital of the Roman Empire, seen as the centre of the 'world'. After the conversion of Constantine, 315 A.D., the bishop of Rome was recognised as the first Bishop of the Christian Church.

g) Historically the great division in the Church between East and West came as a result of the Emperor moving from Rome to Constantinople and the claim of the Bishop of Constantinople to be the first Bishop, or at least equal in authority with the See of Rome.

h) The role of the Pope as Bishop of Rome and first Bishop in the Church has had a long and varied history. He is the visible sign of authority and unity within the Church, acting never independent of, but always in consultation with, the whole body of the Church. He represents for Catholics the sign of unity and authority of the Church. His role as 'visible sign of unity' in the Church was solemnised at the First Vatican Council in 1870 when Papal infallibility was decreed by that Council.

i) In the Second Vatican Council 1962-65, the role of the Pope and Bishops working in collegiality, both for and with the Church, was the dominant development in the truth of the infallibility of both the Pope and the Church.

Some background thoughts on the Church's understanding of infallibility: cf. *Encyclopedia of Theology.* Rahner.

1) Absolute infallibility belongs to God alone.

2) The teaching authority is not above the word of God but is at its service.

3) There is no room for 'Dogmatic imperialism' and 'triumphalism'.

4) It helps the Church to be true to the Gospel.

5) Infallibility of the Church means that the members of the Church join together in mutual service in finding the truth about Jesus.

6) It is also held that, alongside of and outside the scope of the promised and actual infallibility, there can also be human error within the Church. Always be aware of creeping infallibility within the Church.

7) Infallible dogmas are not ultimates but milestones, pointers in the development of Church doctrine.

8) Infallibility is not given to the Church to enable it to transform the 'Good News' into infallible dogmatic propositions.

Exercises

After the input, small groups are formed to react.
Such questions as below might be helpful.

- **What was new?**
- **What was confirmed from the past?**
- **What was unclear?**
- **What do you not agree with?**
- **What do you want to know more about?**

The small groups should then feed back and their findings recorded.

5

Step three: How do our stories touch each other?

In the large group compare the
findings of the two pieces
of paper:

- What have they in common?
- How are they different?
- What light do they shed on
  each other?

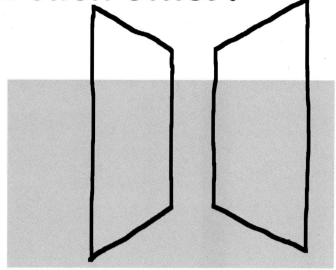

Step four: Prayer time

On a small table place a candle and some oil. Play some music
to create a peaceful, quiet atmosphere. Light the candle.

- Re-read one of the Bible Stories.
- Pray a prayer. Sing a hymn.
- Invite the group to consider how they feel called to
  change as a result of this discussion.

Step five: To talk over with a Catholic friend or sponsor

My reactions, my thoughts and feelings about this issue.
What I like, dislike, don't understand, want to know more about.
How I feel called to look at it from a new angle.

☐ of someone to give us strong leadership.

☐ I am anxious about him telling me how to live my life.

☐ we need one person to unite all the different peoples.

☐ of Pope John Paul II and like his personable approach.

☐ of Pope John Paul II and find him a bit like a superstar.

☐ of why he doesn't sell more of the Church's riches.

☐ of the doctrine of infallibility which I don't really understand.

☐ of something else which strikes me.

In pairs share your responses.

6

Catholics and Confession

Step one: My Story

Recap the previous session and deal briefly with comments and feedback.

Ask them to tick whatever box they want. Value all their responses whatever they are.

Agree/Disagree with the following (mark tick, cross or question mark in each box)

When I think of confession I

☐	can't understand why I cannot just say sorry to God.
☐	wonder what you actually do.
☐	wonder what the priest will think of me.
☐	wonder whether I will get tongue tied and embarrassed.
☐	feel attracted by the promise of healing and growth.
☐	think it represents the hardest part for me about becoming a Catholic.
☐	something else which strikes me.

In pairs share your responses. A leader then records the groups' responses.

(Copy of this questionnaire for photocopying on page 42)

Reflecting on my story

A leader then invites the group to reflect upon their responses. Sometimes he or she might share their own reflections to enable the group to understand what is being asked. The leader might ask such questions as:

> **Who are the people**
> **What are the events, experiences** } **that have led you to give these**
> **What is the reading, media coverage** } **responses?**

Again, this can be discussed in pairs and then gathered together. A further question might then be :

What would be your ideal of confession?
How would it best be for you ?

Step two: The Catholic Community Story

A leader speaks for 5 -10 minutes on the most pertinent elements of this story. The notes below are intended as *background* and not as a verbatim 'talk'.

The Bible and Tradition
Confession/Reconciliation

Sin in the world of the Bible is seen both as individual and social – both personal and universal. The root cause of sin is identified as idolatry, following the way of falsehood rather than the way of truth. The Bible has a large variety of images which seek to express the reality of sin: to go astray; to miss the mark; to be twisted; to be bent; carry a hump; to err; to rebel; to harden the heart; to walk by; to close one's eyes.

One of the greatest signs of sin in the Bible is to be a leper; cast out from the community; forced to live outside the camp; unclean.

Sin and sickness of all kinds are seen as mutually dependent: to raise somebody up; to unbind a person; to let them see; to walk without a limp. All of these are signs of the forgiveness of sin and the reconciling of a person to the community.

"Go and show yourselves to the priest" says Jesus to the lepers, i.e. be reconciled with the community. Jesus was the one who reconciled people, made them whole again and challenged the community to accept the power of being reconcilers. Often his actions led to 'grumbling or murmuring among the crowds'.
cf. Luke 13: 10-17 Jesus and the Woman bent double
 Luke 19: 1-10 Jesus and Zacchaeus

In the writings of Paul we are told that God through Christ has given us the ministry of reconciliation ... and entrusted to us the message of reconciliation ... made us ambassadors of reconciliation, 2 Cor. 5:16-21.

This gift and call to be reconcilers was given to the whole Church. Throughout the ages the exercise of this gift has been sacramentally celebrated by the Church. It has been called :
 The Sacrament of Penance
 The Sacrament of Confession
 The Sacrament of Reconciliation

While all names carry a truth and emphasis on aspects of this gift of healing, the one which is most emphasised today is reconciliation.

Because sin is both personal and social the Church has always emphasised the importance both of the need for a personal and a social expression of sorrow. While it is important to acknowledge to 'God alone' my sorrow and intention of living a different way of life, it is also necessary, because we are a Church and not just a group of individuals, to express our sorrow to the community and to be reconciled by the community.

The way in which the Church celebrates this is as follows:

a) Rite of Reconciliation with an individual and a priest (representing the community).

b) Communal Celebration involving a fairly large community with the possibility of individual absolution.

c) General Absolution.

Exercises

After the input, small groups are formed to react.
Such questions as below might be helpful.

- **What was new?**
- **What was confirmed from the past?**
- **What was unclear?**
- **What do you not agree with?**
- **What do you want to know more about?**

The small groups should then feed back and their findings recorded.

Step three: How do our stories touch each other?

In the large group compare the findings of
the two pieces of paper:

What have they in common?
How are they different?
What light do they shed on each other?

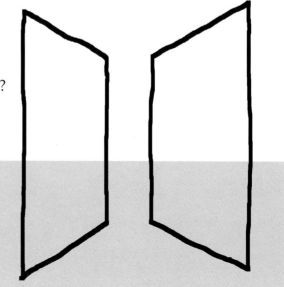

Step four: *Prayer time*

On a small table place a candle and some oil. Play some music to create a peaceful, quiet atmosphere. Light the candle.

- **Re-read one of the Bible Stories.**
- **Pray a prayer. Sing a hymn.**
- **Invite the group to consider how they feel called to change as a result of this discussion.**

Step five: *To talk over with a Catholic friend or sponsor*

- My reactions, my thoughts and feelings about this issue.
- What I like, dislike, don't understand, want to know more about.
- How I feel called to look at it from a new angle.

*Make notes here......ADAPT! ....
these materials!
They are not intended to be placed into inquirers
hands as they stand! Make your own handouts.
cut out. add...Read the Guidelines and the
background carefully – these are intended only
for your use. ADAPT!*

When I think of confession I

☐ can't understand why I cannot just say sorry to God.

☐ wonder what you actually do.

☐ wonder what the priest will think of me.

☐ wonder whether I will get tongue tied and embarrassed.

☐ feel attracted by the promise of healing and growth.

☐ think it represents the hardest part for me about becoming a Catholic.

☐ something else which strikes me.

In pairs share your responses.

Catholics and Mary
Step one: My Story

Recap the previous session and deal briefly with comments, observations and feedback.

Agree/Disagree with the following (mark tick, cross or question mark in each box)

When I think of Mary, the mother of Jesus:

I feel attracted to her because she was a woman and a mother.

I feel puzzled when people pray to her.

I sometimes look at her statue in the church.

I feel attracted to her because she always said "Yes" to God.

I don't know what to think because I don't know what makes her special.

I would like to learn to pray the Hail Mary and the Rosary.

I think she comes across as too good to be true.

I sometimes get the impression that Catholics worship her.

I am interested by her because she saw her Son live, die and rise again.

something else about her which strikes me.

In pairs share your responses. A leader then records the groups' responses.

(Copy of this questionnaire for copying on page 47)

Reflecting on my story

A leader then invites the group to reflect upon their responses. Sometimes he or she might share their own reflections to enable the group to understand what is being asked. The leader might ask such questions as:

Who are the people
What are the events, experiences } **that have led you to give these**
What is the reading, media coverage } **responses?**

Again this can be discussed in pairs and then gathered together. A further question might then be

What would you like Mary to be for you?
How do you best picture Mary for you?

7

Step two: *The Catholic Community Story*

A leader speaks for 5 -10 minutes on the most pertinent elements of this story. The notes below are intended as *background* and not as a verbatim 'talk'.

The Bible and Tradition

The root of all understanding of, and devotion to, Mary is to be found in the story of the Annunciation: Luke 1: 26-38 'In the sixth month the Angel Gabriel was sent by God to a town in Galilee called Nazareth...'

A *Listen to the words spoken to Mary:*
"Hail, full of Grace."

"Hail" (rejoice) used four times in the Old Testament to point to the Messianic deliverance of Israel – Joel 2: 21; Zeph. 3:14 ; Zech. 9:9 ; Sam.4:21.

"Full of grace" – full of God's gift; full of blessing; full of capacity to reflect God's presence in the world.

"The Lord is with you" statement of fact.
    cf. the Beatitudes of Luke Chapter 6.

"Do not be afraid, you have won God's favour."
    cf. Zeph.3:16

"You are to conceive and bear a son."
    cf. Zeph.3:15-17
    "In your midst"(in your womb) meaning in the midst of the temple.

"You must name him Jesus." (Yahweh Saviour)
    The one who saves.

"The Holy Spirit will come upon you and the power of the Most High will cover you with its shadow."
    cf. Deut.7:21 and 1 Kings 8:1-13
    where the signs of God's dwelling (shekinah) in the midst of his people
      are very plain.

"For nothing is impossible to God."
    cf. Gen. 18:9-15 '"Is anything too hard for the Lord?"

"Let it be to me". – Mary's "Yes"
    Her fiat brings about the incarnation of Jesus.
    The Almighty has done great things for her.

Mary is 'the daughter of Zion', the mother of the Lord.

B In Luke 8: 21 Jesus says that "My mother and my brothers are those who hear the word of God and put it into practice."
In Luke 2: 18-19 we are told that all who heard (of Jesus) wondered at what the shepherds had told them but that Mary kept all these things and pondered them in her heart.
She is the essential disciple of the Lord.

C At the Third Ecumenical Council of Ephesus (where Diana of the Ephesians was once worshipped) in 431 Mary received the greatest title of all: 'Theotokos', Mother of God. This title Mother of God and our Saviour Jesus Christ begins another development in our understanding of the significance of Mary in the Church.
The title 'Mother' was used of Jerusalem by Paul: Cf. Gal.4:26.
The title mother is used of the Church; mother of the faithful.

Mary and the Church are seen as united in their vocation of maternity. The one enables us to understand the other – thus we are given the most recent title: 'Mary, Mother of the Church'.

Spend some time looking at Catholic devotions to Mary.
How to pray the Rosary– meditation rather then mechanics.

Exercises

After such an input, small groups are formed to react.
Such questions as below might be helpful:

● **What was new?**
● **What was confirmed from the past?**
● **What was unclear?**
● **What do you not agree with?**
● **What do you want to know more about?**

The small groups should then feed back and their findings recorded.

Step three: How do our stories touch each other?

In the large group compare the findings of the two pieces of paper:

- **What have they in common?**
- **How are they different?**
- **What light do they shed on each other?**

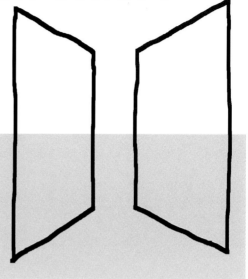

Step four: Prayer time

On a small table place a candle and some oil. Play some music to create a peaceful, quiet atmosphere. Light the candle.

- **Re-read one of the Bible Stories.**
- **Pray a prayer. Sing a hymn.**
- **Invite the group to consider how they feel called to change as a result of this discussion.**

Step five: To talk over with a Catholic friend or sponsor

- My reactions, my thoughts and feelings about this issue.
- What I like, dislike, don't understand, want to know more about.
- How I feel called to look at it from a new angle.

When I think of Mary, the mother of Jesus...

☐ I feel attracted to her because she was a woman and a mother.

☐ I feel puzzled when people pray to her.

☐ I sometimes look at her statue in the church.

☐ I feel attracted to her because she always said "Yes" to God.

☐ I don't know what to think because I don't know what makes her special.

☐ I would like to learn to pray the Hail Mary and the Rosary.

☐ I think she comes across as too good to be true.

☐ I sometimes get the impression that Catholics worship her.

☐ I am interested by her because she saw her Son live, die and rise again.

☐ something else about her which strikes me.

In pairs share your responses.

8 -12
My Treasures: mystery experiences
Introduction and general background: "The in and through approach" to God

Certain events of our lives (birth, love, death,
the struggle against injustice) can bring with them the awareness
that we have a relationship not only to the events themselves
but also to the mystery of life within which they occur.
We can become aware of a fact that we often overlook –
that we come and go within a larger mystery then ourselves.
This way of becoming aware of the Ultimate Mystery
within which "we live and move and have our being"
might be called the **"In and through" approach to God**.
In and through our marriage, our children's growing up,
our own aging, our fight against injustice,
the death of our loved ones, the mystery of life
touches the hearts and minds of those involved.

For most people the communication of God
occurs in and through the ordinary stuff of life
- falling and growing in love
- coping with long term unemployment
- dealing with emotional failure
- feeling united with others in the struggle against injustice
- making a living and building a family

These can be some of the experiences people take
as clues to the goodness rather than the indifferences
of the Mystery of Life. These experiences make us realise
not that there is a Mystery but that we are bonded to that Mystery.
This bond is "given" to us, "comes" to us,
"jumps out" of our lives. Meaning somehow arrives.
We receive it more than make it for ourselves.
At these times of life we are not clever detectives
finding hidden clues –
instead the Mystery unveils itself to us.
It's the Mystery that's on the make, not us.

A favourite story about the contrast between
the "in and through" approach and "the split world" approach
to God is the tale of the old man and the young priest.
It is the late fifties and the Russians have put a man in space.
On his return the cosmonaut informs the world
that he has been to the house of God and no one was at home;
he has been to the far reaches of space
and no God greeted him.
The old man on Chicago's Westside is perturbed about this
and consults the newly ordained priest.
"What about what this Commie said?"
The priest, fresh from a reading of Paul Tillich,
explains that heaven is really a symbol for the transcendence
of God. God does not literally live in the sky.
God is present everywhere, and we use the symbol of the sky
to talk about the transcendent Mystery of God.
"Ha," said the old man with a disgusted look on his face,
"The son of a bitch didn't fly high enough."
(J. Shea. Stories of Faith p.98)

8

My treasures
Step one: *My Story*
Running this session

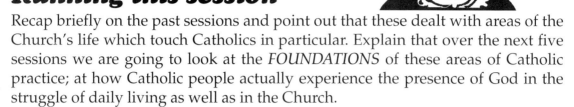

Recap briefly on the past sessions and point out that these dealt with areas of the Church's life which touch Catholics in particular. Explain that over the next five sessions we are going to look at the *FOUNDATIONS* of these areas of Catholic practice; at how Catholic people actually experience the presence of God in the struggle of daily living as well as in the Church.

To break the ice it might be best if a catechist brings some of their own photos and starts off by showing them and talking a little about them. Notice the emphasis on feelings and not just on thinking. People normally talk about the "good" feelings the photos arouse. A catechist or priest might show the group that it is possible to acknowledge "mixed" feelings in this group. It might be that the Scripture Story onwards needs a session of its own. Introduce it by speaking about your own discovery of treasure, i.e. finding out that God isn't in the sky but in your daily living.

Make sure you have a small table cloth, candle, and flowers for the prayer.

Who are the people you keep photos of at home?

In the frames write the names of the people they bring to mind.

Each picture evokes memories of
– people, places, events, good times, sad times.
They are all part of you. They helped to form the kind of person you are now.

50

The pictures contain elements of your story.
Highlight important moments you want to remember.
Describe your pictures to the person next to you for a few minutes.

NOW Some personal stories.
1. Which of the pictures has a story behind it?
Photo of your son/daughter's birth, school photo, retirement, wedding etc... Put a tick beside it.

Which of the pictures would you like to have with you now? Mark it with another tick.

Spend a few moments writing down words, memories, events evoked by recalling the photographs and objects.

Put an X beside the frame that is particularly special to you.

2. Recall the pictures and the objects again and write down the feeling that each evoked.

3. For a few minutes share *as little* or *as much* as **you** wish with the person next to you as to why these photos or objects are important....

In groups of 3 or 4 each person shares. Try to be sensitive to each other.
Notice the threads that are similar, feelings evoked etc...as each person shares.

For the last three or four minutes in the group, choose someone to write down on a large piece of paper some of the events, words, feelings, that were common.

EVENTS	WORDS	FEELINGS
?	?	?

Come together again in the full group, and on a large sheet of paper, record the findings.

Take a few minutes to reflect on what you have written.
What do they say to you about people?

It must be about time for........

8

Step two: The Scripture Story

Listen to the parables of the Treasure and the Pearl: Matthew 13:44-46

Reflect on the story for a few minutes – and then jot down your responses to these questions:

1. What treasures have you found in your life?

2. What did you have to give up to find them?

3. As your life has progressed, have you found new treasures?

4. Does the story speak to some of the feelings and events you have been sharing?

Share your responses with two or three others for a few minutes.

The leader of the evening records the findings on a large piece of paper.

Step three: How do our stories touch each other?

....reflect on both sheets for a few minutes.

....What do the stories of our photos and our treasures have in common?

....How are they different?

....What light do they shed on each other?

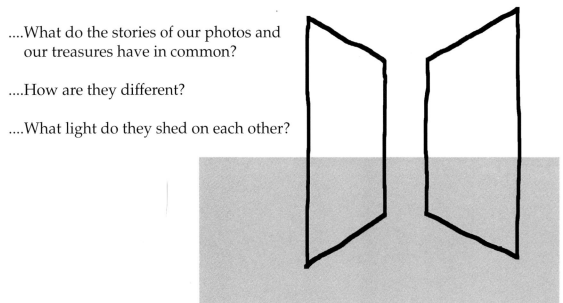

Step four: Liturgy

One person reads again Matthew 13:44-46

Period of Quiet
Hymn: Choose a hymn that reflects the evening's sharing, eg.
Do not be afraid
Abba, Father
Bind us together, Lord

Go back to your photographs
Gather together now in one large photo all the people who are part of your story.
Pray with confidence to God who is Father of all and cares for all his children.

Our Father...

Sign of Peace: Offer each other a sign of peace and friendship.

Let us Pray: God our Father, we give thanks for all the gifts of your creation and the continual life that you give us. We bring before you all those who are dear to us, our families, friends and those who are searching for a new vision of life. May all of us be set free from all that binds in slavery, that we may walk in the light of truth and love. We make this prayer through your Son, Jesus Christ, our Lord. AMEN

May the Lord bless us, and bring us safely to our homes.

Step five: To talk over with a Catholic friend or sponsor

What happened to you when you told your stories?

What did you learn about yourself in retelling your stories?

Have a good week.

9
What changes us
General background

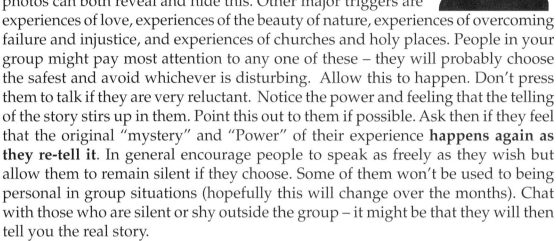

The two major triggers for our experience of living within a greater Mystery are **birth** and **death**. Notice how peoples' photos can both reveal and hide this. Other major triggers are experiences of love, experiences of the beauty of nature, experiences of overcoming failure and injustice, and experiences of churches and holy places. People in your group might pay most attention to any one of these – they will probably choose the safest and avoid whichever is disturbing. Allow this to happen. Don't press them to talk if they are very reluctant. Notice the power and feeling that the telling of the story stirs up in them. Point this out to them if possible. Ask then if they feel that the original "mystery" and "Power" of their experience **happens again as they re-tell it**. In general encourage people to speak as freely as they wish but allow them to remain silent if they choose. Some of them won't be used to being personal in group situations (hopefully this will change over the months). Chat with those who are silent or shy outside the group – it might be that they will then tell you the real story.

Step one: My Story
Running this session

Recap the previous session about photos, treasures and the realisation that we live within a larger Mystery. The recapping will be helped by the ticking of boxes which forms part of this first section. **This recapping of the previous session is important every week.** It links things together, warms people up and allows for feedback. Tell the stories without labouring them. Ask which they liked most. Leave it if the stories don't "register". The footprints are much more personal and need more time and sensitivity. If a catechist introduced them by talking of one of their own footprints it might be easier for the inquirers to find their own. For the Scripture Story you might tell the Jewish story below and then retell Matthew 13:44. Once again you might need a separate session for the Scripture Story onwards.

There was a poor rabbi who lived in the city of Krakow. He lived on the street of the Lost Angel, in the last hovel on that street, with his wife and his four children. Since he was extremely poor, he dreamed every night of riches. But one night the dream was exceptionally vivid. He dreamt that underneath a bridge in the city of Warsaw there was a treasure. When he awoke in the morning, he excitedly told his wife and his children about his dream. He then packed food and clothes and set off for the long journey to find that bridge, unearth that treasure, and be rich. He travelled many long days and long nights and finally arrived at Warsaw. It was just as the dream had pictured it, except for one thing. There was a guard on the bridge, a sentinel who paced back and forth. And so the rabbi, tired from his journey, fell asleep in the bushes. When he awoke, he rattled the bushes with his arm, and the guard spun on him; "You there, come here". He was a simple man so he did not run. He sheepishly came forward. The guard said, "What are you doing here?" Being a simple man who would not run, he was also a simple man who would not lie. He said: "I have dreamed that underneath this bridge there is a treasure and I have travelled many long miles to find that treasure and be rich". The guard said, "That is strange! Just last night I, too, had a dream. I have dreamt that in the city of Krakow, on the street, where lives a rabbi and his wife and their four children there is buried behind the fireplace a treasure. And I leave tonight to find it and be rich."

(J.Shea.Stories of Faith p. 112)

Think back to last weeks' photographs and tick the boxes below that apply to you.

The photos remind me of:
- *birth/death*
- *love/care*
- *holy places*
- *beauty of nature*
- *.............................*

Share your thoughts/feelings about your photographs with the person next to you for a few minutes.

Now some stories
1. Giving birth

"When Catherine, my first child, was born I was anxious because the doctors said it would be a difficult delivery and I was extremely worried about my wife Gill. Then the nurse handed me this little bundle and for ten minutes I just looked at her and held her in my arms. After that I could not have given her away for anything."

2. Growing Up

"I remember walking along one day when I was about fifteen – a summer day when it seemed that school would never end. Suddenly a small toddler, running from his sister, crashed straight into me as his mother shouted, 'Mind that man!' Her words hit me harder than her son. I suddenly saw myself, for the first time, not as a schoolboy, but as a man."

3. Holy Places

"You might find this strange, I sometimes go into the church on my own. I like the church to be empty – for some reason that I don't know I feel united with God and even with all the other people who come to church. I get a sense of peace and quiet that I don't feel when the church is full. I never leave without lighting a candle."

4. The Wonder of Nature

"The first time I climbed to the top of the mountain, looked over the other mountains and down the valley, with its steep sides and three lakes – I felt overwhelmed by a sense of the power and might of nature and smallness of myself. And yet I was part of all this too. It was a strange feeling of being tiny and yet of having accomplished something great."

Spend a few moments alone reflecting on these stories... What did each say to you?

- What did the story of giving birth say to you?
- The story of discovering adulthood?
- The story of visiting the church?
- The story of the mountain?

Turn to the person next to you now and share these reflections.

Then, on your own again, answer the following questions...

1. Do all of these experiences remind you of times when you felt part of something bigger, which was hard to put into words? On the footprints below recall some of those times.

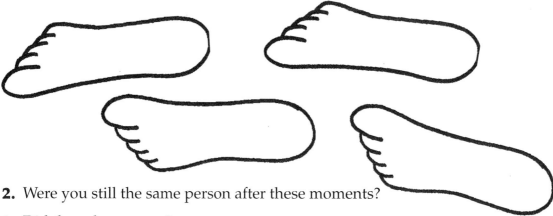

2. Were you still the same person after these moments?

3. Did they change you?

4. Does that change still affect you?

In groups of three or four share your responses to the stories and questions. For the last three or four minutes in the group choose someone to write down on a large sheet of paper some of the words, feelings, events that were common. Then share your findings in the large group.

It must be about time for ....

Step two: The Scripture Story

Much of our lives is taken up with work, children, the house, money, food,...... Sometimes it's hard to see what's happening below the surface. Hopefully these four stories point us in that direction. They catch hold of the depth of some of our everyday experiences; they talk about times we feel part of a greater mystery.

The Christian tradition calls this greater mystery God. It tells us that it is in and through our own experience of life that we touch God, who is the larger mystery within which we all "live and move and have our being".

You might tell the Jewish story on page 54 and then retell the parable of the Treasure and the Pearl: Matthew 13:44-46

Step three: How do the stories touch each other?

1. In hearing and telling the stories tonight have you discovered anything about finding the hidden treasure or the pearl of great price?

2. Have you found that some of the ordinary experiences in your life are in fact "religious"?

In groups of three or four share your responses to these questions. In the large group bring together the main threads of the evening.

Step four: Liturgy

Let us pray:
Loving Father, you invite us through your Son, Jesus, to experience the fullness of life. We thank you for the world in which we live. We thank you for the beauty of creation, for the people who have enriched our lives by their love. We thank you for all the stories we have shared. We ask this through Jesus Christ our Lord. AMEN.

Reading: Matthew 13:44-46

Period of Quiet

Hymn: Choose a hymn that reflects this evening's sharing: eg.
I will be with you wherever you go
How great is our God
Christ be beside me

Turn to the person next to you. Make the sign of the cross on his/her forehead and say:
(Name): I thank you for the way your story speaks to me of God.

Final Blessing: Out of his infinite goodness may God give us the grace for our hidden self to grow strong, and feel the call to freedom he is inviting us to share through Jesus Christ our Lord.   AMEN.

Step five: To talk over with a Catholic friend or sponsor

What happened to you when you told and listened to the stories?

What did you learn about yourself in retelling your stories?

10

Experiences of conversion

General background

"God" is the word people call out when they come into contact with the greater than they are. A child is born and the religious person exclaims "God". In health or sickness the religious person shouts "God". We die and our lips whisper "God". When we are reduced to slavery and then rise against whoever oppresses us and discover a new freedom the religious person exclaims "God". We look at the hills and say "Oh God, how beautiful". We do not see God. We see hills, water, colour, shapes. It is in the connection between myself and scenery that I am triggered into an awareness of the greater mystery I live within. I acknowledge that awareness by calling "God". The "in and through" approach always keeps the presence of God joined to the presence of our everyday world. In and through our love for one another we become aware of a greater love which supports and encourages us. In this way God, ourselves and others are permanently bound together. We cannot talk about our relationship with God without talking about our other relationships – and we can't talk about our ordinary relationships at any depth without talking about our relationship to God. The experience behind the phrase "God is Love" is invariably a human relationship which is so loving and a source of love so beyond us that people involved call out, "God is love".

The "in and through" approach begins with a belief and expectation of divine presence everywhere – not at special times, with special people, in special places. The question is not how to make the missing God present but how the everpresent God touches us here. Faith is not believing in what cannot be seen but responding in heart and mind to what cannot be escaped – both love and suffering.

Step one: My Story
Running this session

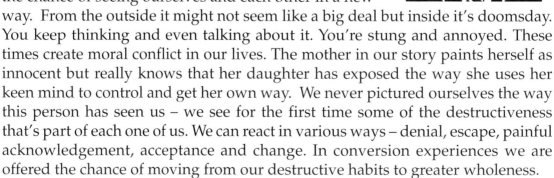

Conversion experiences involve both love and suffering. They are the times our hearts are laid bare and we're given the chance of seeing ourselves and each other in a new way. From the outside it might not seem like a big deal but inside it's doomsday. You keep thinking and even talking about it. You're stung and annoyed. These times create moral conflict in our lives. The mother in our story paints herself as innocent but really knows that her daughter has exposed the way she uses her keen mind to control and get her own way. We never pictured ourselves the way this person has seen us – we see for the first time some of the destructiveness that's part of each one of us. We can react in various ways – denial, escape, painful acknowledgement, acceptance and change. In conversion experiences we are offered the chance of moving from our destructive habits to greater wholeness.

- from self-elevation to being finite and limited
- from powerlessness to being able to act
- from narrowness of life to a greater fullness in living.

Recap the previous session and deal briefly with comments, observations and feedback. Introduce "The God I believe in"; emphasise that there are no right and wrong answers here and so people should feel free to tick whatever they really think and feel. Don't judge any of their responses – let them ride and point out the variety, richness and validity of each angle. Tell the two stories and gather reactions. Plenty of time should be given to the question about times we've personally been hit for six. When introducing the Scripture Story a catechist might share a time when they've felt some of the struggles the young man experiences. Once again it might be found that this session needs to be split into two sessions.

The God I believe in

(Agree, Disagree, tick, cross or question mark in each box)

When I think of God I think of:

- going to church
- being in love
- being watched
- the deepest part of me
- Jesus
- as a mystery touching my life
- as a caring Father
- as the one who challenges my way of life
- ....

In pairs share your responses. The leader records the groups' responses.

(Copy of this questionnaire for photocopying on page 63)

Now some stories

1. "You know what happened to me the other night. Well, we've been having trouble with our daughter. She's so inconsiderate. I woke up at 1am. She still wasn't in, although she was supposed to be home for midnight. When she came in I was determined to keep my cool, to sit down with her and tell her how much her father and I worried about where she might be, or what might have happened. Well, I sat her down and told her that. You know what she said in reply, 'How come every time we sit down and have one of these little chats *you* always come out looking so good?'"

2. "When one of my neighbours came round with a petition requesting the council to remove a group of itinerants from our area and give them a proper campsite – I signed it.

Later that evening, watching the news on T.V., I was angry when the reports on South Africa were shown. Suddenly I found myself saying out loud 'Dear God - I did it myself earlier tonight'. I was really shook up for a few days by that ....By the time I'd picked up courage to take my name off the list it had been sent to the council. Mind you, I feel more sympathy for the whites in South Africa now. It will take real courage for them to change. Maybe we're all prejudiced in some way or other."

What did the story of the mother and daughter say to you?

....

....

What did the story about the itinerants say to you?

....

....

Turn to the person next to you and share.

Then on your own again answer the following questions:

1. Can you remember any times when you were hit for six by what somebody said to you about yourself?

2. How did you react?

	forgot about it
	made excuses for yourself
	saw yourself in a new light
	did something about it

Tick which apply

Share in groups of three or four – then share your groups' findings in the large group and record them on a large piece of paper.

Step three: The Scripture Story

Listen to the story of the Young Man: *Matthew 19: 16-22*

1. Have you ever felt like the young man in the story?

2. What was so uncomfortable about Jesus' reply?

3. Is there anything you think you will have to give up if you become a Catholic?

4. Have there been times when you've known what you really wanted to do but haven't done it?

5. Can you remember times when you've had to change the way you paint yourself as innocent and others guilty?

In groups of three or four share your responses to these questions. In the large group, the leader records your findings on a piece of paper.

Step three: *How do our stories touch each other?*

In the large group compare the findings of the two pieces of paper.

● What have they in common?
● How are they different?
● What light do they shed on each other?

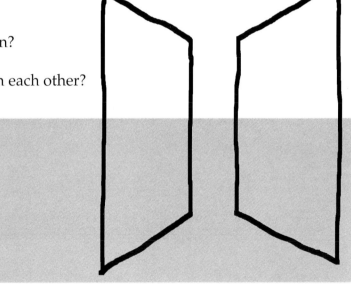

Step four: *Liturgy*

On a small table place a candle and some oil. Play some music to create a peaceful, quiet atmosphere. Light the candle.

Let us pray:
Leader:
Heavenly Father, we believe that we are your children.
We give thanks for your wisdom in making us all different,
yet dependent on each other. Help us to recognise the barriers and
divisions that we have allowed to blind us from seeing your creative work in the
people and events around us. Give us the courage to change, and the grace to

trust that your love will continually sustain us. We make this prayer through your Son, Jesus Christ our Lord.

All: Amen

Reading: Matthew 19:16-22

Blessing of the oil

Leader:
May the Lord bless this oil. May it be for us a sign of strength and blessing, in the name of the Father and the Son and the Holy Spirit.

The leader makes the sign of the cross on the hands of each person, praying:
Name, may you always be open to hearing the call of Christ in your life.

Now let us offer each other a sign of peace and friendship.

Final Blessing: May Almighty God bless us, and bring us to a new vision of his love and care for us, through his Son, Jesus Christ our Lord.
Amen.

Step five: To talk over with your sponsor

- what tonight was like for you.
- your own experience of change and conversion.

Have a good week.

The God I believe in

When I think of God I think of...

(Agree, Disagree, tick, cross or question mark in each box)

☐ going to church

☐ being in love

☐ being watched

☐ the deepest part of me

☐ Jesus

☐ as a mystery touching my life

☐ as a caring Father

☐ as the one who challenges my way of life

☐ ....

In pairs share your responses.

11

Impact experiences
General background: Tradition

On our journey of faith we don't travel alone. We walk with others. We also remember the journeys of those who came before us. We travel with **Tradition** as guide. The Church *begins* with people sharing their revelations of God and their journeys of faith. Tradition is basically the record of other peoples' revelations of God and journeys of faith. Tradition includes the Bible, the lives of the saints, liturgical practices, the history of the Church, the teaching of the Pope and bishops of the Church, etc. We are helped to see all this in order of importance – the Church, for example, gives a special place to the Bible, especially the **New Testament**. The linking of our lives to the Tradition often takes the form of a dialogue with the *Bible*. (So we have a Scripture story in each session)

In this conversation between the contemporary experience of living and Tradition there are two fundamental moves.

1. We search the Tradition for experiences which correct and provoke us. Of course we're never neutral in this search – we consult the Tradition out of selective interests. These interests can act as filters, allowing in whatever seems friendly and blocking whatever appears either irrelevant or threatening. Current interest in social injustice picks out the story of the Jewish people in Egypt, the wanderings through the desert to the Promised Land, and the clash between Jesus and the Scribes and Pharisees and examines them to see if they have anything to say to our concerns.

2. The second movement is that the Tradition *talks back.* For the most part it says "Yes but..." It affirms the insights and values that are genuinely Christian but enriches them with other perspectives. Normally, it criticizes them by expansion. To the Charismatics it says: "Yes, prayer should be joyful, personal, expressive but what was it again that the prophets and Jesus said about 'religious practices'?" To the 'justice and peaceniks' it says: "Yes, we must be actively engaged in the social and economic spheres of life but this involvement stems from belief in God and this means we should enter the struggle in a distinctive way."

So in this dialogue between personal experience and Tradition (the first four movements in these materials) experience selects, Tradition responds and conversations begin to develop – ultimately towards living and acting more fully in Jesus Christ.

Step one: My Story
Running this session

3. Impact experiences are the times we've remembered, thought about and re-told which have now yielded for us a truth of life: "This is how life really is..." We tell these

stories time and time again until we finally get them right. Our friends tell us they've heard it before – they have on the surface, but *we ourselves haven't.* There's still more in the experience than we've understood or put into words. So these times reverberate and ripple into our lives. It takes time to unearth what's really happened to us in this event. What counts is what's really happened to us personally – its inner impact on us – what's happened inside us. The teacher would say that the truth about life that his experience of Derek and Joe yielded was that "People can change, but only at a cost, which is usually paid by other people." In religious language he would say "God caught Derek in Joe" or "I wanted to excommunicate Derek but Joe stayed with him in his sin." The teacher tells the story so that he himself is helped in the moral conflicts of his own life – he has to face Derek and others like him every day.

4. Begin the session by recapping upon the previous session and allowing for brief comments. Once again when using the boxes tell people to tick or cross honestly without thinking too long. The statements are intended as examples of some of the common "truths" of life by which we live. The significant thing is what personal experience is behind each statement. Encourage people to say when they discovered this to be true or false for themselves.

Tell the story of Derek and Joe and allow different interpretations. Perhaps a catechist could personally introduce the section of "What people, Life, God, is like". Similarly the Scripture Story of the woman and the lost coin could be prefaced by a personal sharing to help people think for themselves.

Agree/Disagree (Mark tick, cross or question mark in each box)

☐	People are like leopards, they never change their spots
☐	Life is hard and unfair
☐	You've got to look after number one
☐	Charity begins at home
☐	You can't take people at face value
☐	God likes the sinner best
☐	People do change – but at a cost
☐	There's no point helping lame ducks

Share in pairs. The leader then records the groups' responses.

(Copy of this questionnaire for photocopying on page 69)

Now a Personal Story

"I wasn't sure whether we should have taken Derek or not but I eventually gave in to his parents' pleading. School trips always have their problems but this time they started early. By the time we got unpacked Emily had lost her purse, Jonathan his new penknife, and David a five pound note. The purse and the knife and the five pound note were found in Derek's locker. When I asked him why he did it he denied it and stared at me blankly.

11

I was all for sending him home and was arranging to do so as I started to tell the warden. He said we should give Derek to Joe for the week. Joe was a retired miner, the gardener, plumber and handyman. I gave in, thinking it would never work. The next morning at 7.30 am Joe arrived and asked me which one Derek was. He woke him up saying, "Come now. I need you. There's lots of work to be done."

In the next four days wherever you saw Joe you saw Derek. Whenever you saw Derek you saw Joe: planting, mowing, painting, fixing. The day we all knew would come came and the coach appeared on the drive – we waited for Derek as he walked alongside Joe. Derek was allowing Joe to put his arm around his waist and there was a spring in each step. The young lad, who had lost out on so much in his brief life, was a new person – he was like someone who had finally found a coin that had vanished so long ago."

1. Does the story make you smile?

2. Which of the characters do you warm to most?

3. What do you think each of them has learnt from the experience?

4. What makes the teacher tell the story time and time again?

Take some time to answer these questions on your own then share with the person next to you. Then on your own again answer the following questions:

1. Think of times in your life when you've felt you've discovered something important about

    a) what people are like?

    b) what life is like?

    c) what God is like?

2. Can you remember telling and retelling the stories of these experiences to your friends? Did you gain new insights in the telling?

3. Do you find that any of these stories help you with some of the struggles and conflicts you face now?

Share in three's or four's. Then the leader records the findings on a large white piece of paper.

Step two: *The Scripture Story*

Listen to the story of the woman and the lost coin: Luke 15:8-10

1. Have you ever felt lost?

2. Who "searched thoroughly" for you?

3. Have you ever written somebody off?

4. Did anything happen to make you change your mind?

5. Is God "miserly" because he won't let even one person be lost?

Answer these questions on your own then share in three's and four's and then in the large group the leader records the findings on a large piece of paper.

Step three: How do our stories touch each other?

Looking at two pieces of paper notice what's similar, what's different, and what light they shed on each other.

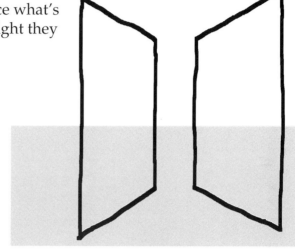

Step four: Liturgy

Place a Paschal Candle in the centre.
See that each person present has a
small candle.

Leader: Let us Pray:

Heavenly Father, you sent your Son, Jesus, to be the light of the world and to show us the way to you. Take away from us all that prevents your light shining in our lives. Bring life and light to all that is dark, so that we may become visible signs of your love and compassion in the world. We ask this through your Son, Jesus Christ, who is the light of the world.

All: Amen.

Reading: Luke 15:8-10

The leader takes a candle and lights it from the Paschal Candle. Each person is handed a lighted candle by the leader saying:

(Name) May you bring the light of Christ to all you meet.

Response: I will, with God's help.

Final Prayer
God our Father, we thank you for the light and life you continually give us through others. May we continue to discover new ways of recognising your light in our life. We ask this through your Son, Jesus Christ our Lord.

All: Amen.

Hymn: Choose a hymn that reflects tonight's discussion.

Step five: To talk over with your sponsor

● What happened for you tonight?

● Was this the presence of God?

● When have you felt life has been telling you something?

*Make notes here......ADAPT! ....
these materials!
They are not intended to be placed into inquirers
hands as they stand! Make your own handouts,
cut out, add...Read the Guidelines and the
background carefully — these are intended only
for your use. ADAPT!*

Agree/Disagree (Mark tick, cross or question mark in each box)

☐ People are like leopards, they never change their spots

☐ Life is hard and unfair

☐ You've got to look after number one

☐ Charity begins at home

☐ You can't take people at face value

☐ God likes the sinner best

☐ People do change - but at a cost

☐ There's no point helping lame ducks

12

Stormy times
General background

The "in and through" approach to God gives us such pictures as friend, companion and pilgrim. Sometimes, however, this picture of friendship and closeness can go badly wrong. It can lead to a sugary "me and my best friend" approach to God. God becomes anything *we* make him. The name God gives for himself in the Book of Exodus 3:14 can be translated in many ways. One of the most provocative is: "I will be with you as who I am will I be with you". The journey of faith is not any old life – with God along for the ride.

The divine companion and friend influences and changes our values and perspectives. To have God as a friend is to walk with him as who he is, not as who we want him to be. God is more than a friend and companion on the journey. He is the *path* too! He leads us beyond where we are now. He has a new and different future in store for us. He is a God who *makes storms*: storms which unsettle the limits we set ourselves, the securities we live by, the control we try to exercise over our lives. These storms can be the occasion of painful conversion and change – a different me and you, a new God, a more compassionate or challenging Jesus.

Step one: My Story
Running this session

All that was said about conversion experiences in Session 10 applies here again. Now we try to link conversion more explicitly with the person and life of Jesus. In introducing the session recap the previous meeting on "impact experiences" and talk about the different impacts of Jesus on our lives. The exercise with the boxes is one way of surfacing our different impressions of Jesus. Don't try to give the "right" answers – the Scripture Story will attempt later on to speak to each of our approaches. If you think the story about the woman dying is unsuitable for your group you could go straight into the Scripture Story. A catechist or priest might share a personal experience of storm and its overcoming in order to help people focus on storms in their own lives.

Obviously this is a very sensitive area and it might be possible only to share in twos or threes and not in the larger group. Notice the *personal decisions for the future* Section. An individual interview with each inquirer might be helpful as a guide to deciding whether to carry on to the Rite of Becoming Catechumens. Some general introduction to that Rite needs to be given both to the group and to the Parish Community.

It is possible to celebrate it on the 1st, 2nd or 3rd Sunday of Advent – but preferably before Christmas.

Agree/Disagree (Mark tick, cross or question mark in each box)

	Jesus has all the answers to our problems
	Jesus is a good example of how to live
	Jesus is portrayed as someone who always shops at the local store
	Jesus always knew how things were going to turn out
	Jesus experienced the same fears and pains as us
	Jesus liked some people more than others

Share in pairs. The leader then records the groups' responses.
(Copy of this questionnaire for photocopying on page 74)

Now...a personal story

"When my grandmother was dying I was asked to go and talk with her about where she wanted to be buried. The problem was that the old grave yard was closed and was more than twenty miles away. The new one was near where we lived now.
'How are you?' I asked. 'I'm dying.' she replied.
'I know,' I said. 'They tell me downstairs you want to be buried in the old grave yard. Wouldn't it be better if you were buried here where we can look after the grave?'
She looked at me with a gleam of humour in the eye. 'Who's dying?– you or me? I know more people who are dead than alive and when the resurrection comes I want to be surrounded by my friends.' There was no argument."

1. What does the story say to you?

2. Are you surprised by the woman's confidence in facing death?

3. Where does she get this confidence from?

4. What makes her want to be surrounded by her friends?

Take some time to answer these questions on your own, then share with the person next to you. Then, on your own again, respond to the following:

● Recall a time when you set out to help someone and they ended up helping you.

● Who are the people you want to be surrounded by now?

● Recall a time when you experienced a kind of death and then a resurrection to a new life.

Share in three's or four's. Then the leader records the findings on a large piece of paper.

12

Step two: The Scripture Story

Listen to the story of the calming of the storm: Matthew 8:23-27

1. What is it like to leave dry land and follow someone into a boat? What risks do you have to take? What securities do you leave behind?

2. Have you ever felt "swamped" like the disciples? Who did you call to in your need? Did God seem to be asleep?

3. What were you really afraid of? How was your storm calmed? Were you surprised you came through it? What was this 'strange' power that brought you through?

Answer these questions on your own then share in three's and four's. Then in the large group the leader records the findings on a large piece of paper.

Step three: How do the stories touch each other?

Looking at the two pieces of paper, notice what's similar, what's different, and what light they shed on each other.

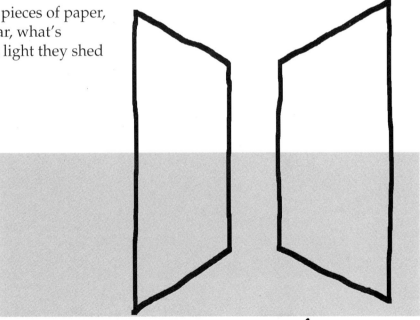

Step four: Liturgy

Play a suitable piece of music to help create a peaceful atmosphere.

Leader:
God our Father, we are surrounded by your wonders and led by the greatness of your plan for us. Your world is a gracious gift filled with love. Give us the eyes to see your hand at work in our daily lives in very ordinary ways and the faith to recognise your guiding hand. We ask this through your Son, Jesus Christ our Lord.

All: Amen.

Reading: Matthew 8: 23-27

The leader invites those present to pray spontaneously for a few moments.

All pray the Our Father.

Priest blesses each person individually–

Name, May the love of God be with you, may the joy of the Risen Christ sustain you, may the power of the Holy Spirit overshadow you all the days of your life.

All: Amen.

Step five: To talk over with your sponsor

What happened for you tonight?

Did you get any new ideas of what it is to be a follower of Jesus?

Personal decisions for the future

We suggest that you now take some time to reflect what these weeks have been like for you?

What have you discovered
- about yourself?
- about God?
- about the Church?

Perhaps you could talk this over with your sponsor, catechist and priest with a view to deciding whether to go forward to the Rite of Welcome and Entry into the Catholic Community.

What Jesus is like...

Agree/Disagree (Mark tick, cross or question mark in each box)

☐ Jesus has all the answers to our problems

☐ Jesus is a good example of how to live

☐ Jesus is portrayed as someone who always shops at the local store

☐ Jesus always knew how things were going to turn out

☐ Jesus experienced the same fears and pains as us

☐ Jesus liked some people more than others

Reclaiming your Baptism & discerning readiness for the Rite of becoming Catechumens

The inquiry groups often include the following broad categories of people:

A Those unbaptised
B Those baptised but not catechised
C Those baptised and belonging to other Christian Churches.

It is suggested that sometime during the inquiry period the explicit faith history of groups B and C in particular is explored. They need to be helped to see their baptism positively so that they don't feel they are 'missing out' when people in category A are baptised.

General questions

Were they brought up in a Christian family?
What was the family atmosphere like?
Were they baptised?
Did they go to church or Sunday school?
Did they ever stop going to church?
What made them want to start again?

Specific Baptism questions

Rather than being satisfied simply by the production of a baptismal certificate, try imaginatively to explore what it expresses. Ask the inquirers to dig into their family history over such questions as:

● Where were your parents living at the time of your baptism?
   What was life like for them?
   What might they have experienced at your birth?
   What might they have hoped for or given thanks for at your baptism?
   What made them give you your name?

● Who were your Godparents?
   Why do you think your parents asked them?
   What has been the relationship between you and them?
   Who was the minister or priest?

What sort of relationship did they have with the family?
What has been your relationship with the Church?

● How did your parents try to live the baptismal promises they made for you? As you grew up how did you (didn't you) make those baptismal promises for yourself?

It is helpful for the catechist or priest to share some of their own faith story on both sets of questions. This is simply with a view to putting the inquirers in touch with their story. Obviously much work could be done in small groups and then shared in the larger group. The session might end with some prayerful symbolic reclaiming of baptism – a blessing with water, a giving of light.

What should we do with the unbaptised inquirer while this is happening with groups B and C? Won't they feel out of it? Yes, they will unless the questions are adapted for them too. Could we ask about their family's relationship with the Church, with the priest or minister; about why they were not baptised? Perhaps, more positively, could we explore who or what has attracted them to the Catholic Church now? Could we ask who their friends in faith are and who they would like for their sponsors and Godparents?

This work of reclaiming our baptism should make it possible to distinguish comfortably between groups A, B, and C, informally in the group sessions and formally in the Rite of Becoming Catechumens and the Rite of Welcome.

Discerning readiness for the Rite of becoming Catechumens & Celebrating the Rite

These are dealt with in some detail in the introductory notes, RCIA BASICS. In the text of Rite of Christian Initiation of Adults paragraphs 13, 18 and 41-47 are especially relevant. See also RCIA Basics (page 18) for notes on distinguishing between those already baptised and those who are unbaptised.

Looking back – Looking forward

This Session can follow the Rite of becoming Catechumens in order to consolidate personal growth and to plan for the future.

1. Reflecting on your experience of the Rite

A How did you feel about being "up there" in front of the larger community of the parish?

B How did you feel when you heard your name called out?

C How did you feel when your sponsor spoke on your behalf?

D How did you feel when your senses were anointed with oil?

E How did you feel about the people of the parish welcoming you and praying for you?

F How did you feel about being called along with other inquirers and about being "dismissed" together?

2. Looking back over 3 months

A What have you discovered
- about yourself?
- about others?
- about God?
- about the Church?

B What has disappointed you, frustrated you, over the past three months?

Allow the inquirers to say what they want – don't get defensive about their disappointments. Talk over the comments in your team meetings.

3. Looking forward – New Year to Lent

Ask the Catechumens what topics, issues, stories they want included over the next three months. Encourage them to be open and honest. It won't be possible to do everything they want but their suggestions can be discussed in the team meetings.

B"This is a time when the catechumens
learn to turn more readily
to God in prayer, to bear witness to the faith,
in all things to keep their hearts set
on Christ...and to practise love of neighbour,
even at the cost of self renunciation.
Thus formed the newly converted
set out on a spiritual journey."*

(Rite)

THE FORMATION PERIOD
(Period of Catechumenate)

Guidelines

These materials are intended for the use of priests and catechists and not for catechumens. They contain themes for six sessions, and some practical individual and group exercises. They should not be used just as they stand because they contain the scriptural and theological background which the priest and catechist needs. Instead, worksheets will need to be made for each session to suit the particular catechumens. In these sessions, as throughout the RCIA process, it is essential to ADAPT, ADAPT, ADAPT.

Clothes for the journey

These materials assume that at every session each member of the group has a Bible and a copy of "How to Survive being married to a Catholic", (Redemptorist Publications). The Sunday Readings for Year B should also be to hand.

Liturgies

The suggested sessions are faithful to the Rite. *(Paragraphs 75-104)* These sections of the Rite should be studied and adapted to the needs of each parish. The Rite of Election is normally celebrated on the First Sunday of Lent.

Length of Catechumenate

The Rite says: "The time spent in the catechumenate period should be long enough – several years if necessary – for the conversion and faith of the catechumens to become strong." *(R.C.I.A. Par. 76)* Beware of rushing things just to be ready for initiation. Take more time when necessary.

Method and timing for each session

Step one: Personal Stories
"How to survive being married to a Catholic"
(Redemptorist Publications) 20 minutes

Step two: Read the Scripture Story 5 minutes

Step three: Initial Reactions to the Scripture Story. 5 minutes

Step four: Input. 10 minutes
Exercises, alone and in groups 30 minutes

Step five: How do the Stories touch? 5 minutes

Step six: The call to change
The intention is to raise the issue rather than suggest instant resolutions. The catechumen and sponsor can in private discuss this part of the meeting. 5 minutes

Step seven: Liturgy
Make sure this is included and given enough time rather than being edged out by all the talking. 15 minutes

Each of the steps is important and necessary but adapt them; change the order or the emphasis to suit the particular group.

Alternative Routes

for the Catechumenate Period

The suggested themes outlined in these Sessions are not intended to be comprehensive; nor is it possible to suggest themes that would include all aspects of the Christian life. There are many areas to be explored and these **"alternative routes"** are proposed, with some possible reading material, to remind readers of other significant themes and to help in the process of discovering the treasures of our Faith.

Life Questions
Building Your Own Conscience:
W J O'Malley,
(Tabor Publishing)
The Road Less Travelled:
M Scott Peck
(Arrow Books)

Sacramental Approach
Introductions to the Rites of Celebrations of the Sacraments

The Sacraments and You:
M Pennock,
(Ave Maria)

History of Salvation – Bible Approach
Discovering the Promise of the Old Testament:
M. Pennock, *(Ave Maria)*
Breaking Open the Gospel of Mark:
G Weber & R Miller, *(St Anthony Messenger)*
Impressions of Jesus: Denis McBride,
(Redemptorist Publications)
The Jesus Story: Wilfrid Harrington,
(Columba)
The Readings of Cycles A, B & C of Church Lectionary

'Fraid so! In the last section we said we are surrounded by mystery. Now there's a word for the mystery which is the source of all things. The word is **God.** Unfortunately many people think of God not as the mysterious source of everything, but as an extra-powerful man in the sky.

Rather like this. . .

Or this. . .

Or this. . .

Or this. . .

Or this. . .

Or this. . .

The trouble with all these pictures is that they're human inventions. They're the result of people making God in their own image.

Well, partly because human beings like to have everything cut and dried. They're uneasy with anything they can't explain; or with anything that can't be weighed and measured.

We saw in the last section how the mystery of the human person defies complete analysis...

REMEMBER ME?

How much more is the mystery we call God beyond our comprehension? But people don't like things to be beyond their comprehension.

WHAT ARE YOU DRAWING, DEAR?

GOD!

BUT NO-ONE KNOWS WHAT GOD LOOKS LIKE.

THEY WILL WHEN I'VE FINISHED THIS!

So people try to tie God down and make him manageable. When they do that there are bound to be distortions, and usually the distortions reflect their own fears and anxieties and guilt.

That's why their pictures of God tend to come out as harsh and authoritarian.

SO WE SHOULDN'T TALK ABOUT GOD AT ALL, THEN?

Well, we can't avoid talking about God. But we should remember that the words we use can never capture the reality of God. Some ways of talking about God are less misleading than others. But even the best is only like a finger pointing. It's not the reality.

LOOK! THE MOON

THAT'S NOT THE MOON, IT'S A FINGER

JUST A MINUTE, THOUGH. IF WE CAN'T PUT GOD INTO WORDS, HOW CAN WE KNOW HIM?

Good question, madam. Catholics (and other Christians) believe that

God has made **himself** known to mankind.

First he revealed himself to the Jewish people — and the story of God's dealings with them is told in the Old Testament. There we see a picture of a God who is merciful, loving and compassionate. He remains faithful to his chosen people, even when they turn away from him.

> "When Israel was a child I loved him, and I called my son out of Egypt...I myself taught Ephraim to walk...I took them in my arms... I led them with reins of kindness, with leading-strings of love. I was like someone who lifts an infant close against his cheek; stooping down to him I gave him his food. *(from the prophet Hosea)*
>
> The Lord is my shepherd I shall not want; he makes me lie down in green pastures. He leads me beside still waters; he restores my soul He leads me in paths of righteousness for his name's sake. *(Psalm 23)*

Christians believe that these sublime images of a loving God were brought to fulfilment in an astounding way. God not only **revealed** himself but **gave** himself to us in a person — Jesus Christ. Not simply words written down, but the Word made flesh.

Jesus doesn't tell us **about** God; he **shows** us God. That's why his life is central to Catholics and to all Christians.

83

Catholics and God
Step one: Personal Story

Spend 5 minutes looking at the cartoons on pages 82-83 from "How to Survive being married to a Catholic". Then on your own respond to the following:

1. Which of the cartoons is the funniest for you?

2. Which of them is most like your own image of God?

3. Which cartoon do you most dislike and would like to change?

In small groups share your responses. Then a leader records the findings in the large group.

Step two: Scripture Story

Listen to the extract from Isaiah 55: 1-11 which is the First Reading for The Baptism of the Lord, Year B.

Step three: Initial reactions to this Story

Which pictures, words, do you remember?
Which part of the story strikes you most?
Which parts of the story don't you understand?

Step four: Input

Background

The Jewish Exile in Babylon (587 – 539 BC), although lasting only 48 years, was one of the most significant events in developing both the Jewish and, later, Christian understanding of God.

This historical tragedy fertilised and deepened the soil of Israel's religious understanding:

a) The Jewish people grow to recognise themselves as a Holy People separated from the Nations by purity of life and submission to God's rule.

b) God is no longer seen as the God of Israel but his purpose spans the ages from the beginning of history to the end. Israel is called to be the agent of God in bringing about the redemption of all.

c) God is active in the lives of all people and history; not just in the past and present but also in the future; a vast expansion of the idea of *hope*. Our future is in the hands of God who has saved us – Exodus – and brought us back from Exile and will save us in the future.

d) A rich imagery is developed which explores the insights which came out of the experience of Exile.
e.g.
- A new Exodus
- A new people
- A new Creation
- A new Garden of paradise
- A new Covenant which would never lapse
- A new heart
- A new Spirit poured out

The function of all this imagery was not simply to describe the fact that God's ways are not our ways or God's thoughts are not our thoughts but to emphasise the fact that because this is the way that God acts and will act in the future – we are called to act this way towards ourselves and others, now and in the future. The simple way of expressing this is that we are called to conversion, i.e. to see the world and to act in the world through the eyes of God and not mammon.

Isaiah 55:1-11
- Offers a vision of the future with a free offer of mercy to all; a new paradise.
- A vision which we are called to make a reality in our lives and in our world.
- This is what God will do for each one of us and for all; this is what we should do for each other as we work for Justice and Peace for all.

We look at Isaiah 55: 1-11 in more detail:
vv 1-2
a) Images of fullness, freedom, plenty, shared out – without money and without price! A full measure, flowing over, shaken together and running over.

b) This is what God is like – bounteous, generous to a fault, utterly free in what he gives.

c) This is what we're called to be: bounteous, generous to a fault, utterly free in giving what's needed. Note the implication of this for Justice and Peace in our world.

vv 3-5
a) God is life giving, faithful – for all peoples.

b) We are called to *listen* (Shema, Israel) to the words and actions of God – to be witnesses to this, to be life givers, faithful for all peoples.

vv 6-9

a) Call to seek the Lord – return to him in *conversion.*

b) God is abundant in mercy and pardon – unlike the ways of the world.

c) My thoughts not your thoughts, etc. This is not in the sense of the transcendent, untouchable God but in the sense of the call to be abundant in mercy and pardon; making the ways of God present in our world.

vv 10-11

a) Images of growth, harvest, riches, life-giving, unstoppable. The word of life is the word of God.

b) The word of God is formed in its fullest expression in Jesus – "You are my beloved Son in whom I am well pleased". *(Mark 1:11)* Jesus above all lives out the reality of God's incredible richness, growth, life-giving generosity, faithfulness, abundant mercy and pardon. He is life giving in every situation.

c) The word of God – the call to be all these things – continues to live in each one of us – seeking and desiring to become a constant reality.

The whole of Isaiah 55:1-11 in our terms involves a deep call to work and live Justice and Peace because that is what God is about.

Exercises

1. Break up the text into 3 sections, one of which might prove enough to look at today.

   a) Verses 1-5
   b) Verses 6-9
   c) Verses 10-11

Make a list of the ways in this story that God is close to his people.

2. a) Complete the table on page 87 individually then share in small groups.
   b) Discuss the following questions in the larger group:

- What happens between God and David? What then happens to the people?
- Is what God calls his people to do realistic?
- Is it realistic for God to expect me to be lifegiving in the situations of my own life?

How God is close to his People	What God promises his People	What we're called to be

Step five: How do the stories touch each other?

Compare the findings from the cartoons with the findings from Isaiah. Are they similar? How are they different?

Step six: The call to change

This is the most difficult of the steps. The intention is to raise the issue rather than to make instant resolutions. This should be the main issue for conversations between catechumen and sponsor outside of the sessions.

As a result of these stories and sharing how do I feel called to change?

Step seven: Liturgy

Focus on the Bible. Place it or the Lectionary in a central place and surround it with flowers and candles. Begin by playing some soft music.

15

Prayer

God our Father, you have been speaking to us since the beginning of time. You made the covenant of love with your people Israel and called David to be your witness to all nations. You ask us now to listen, to listen to you so that our souls will live.

Catechist: For all that God does in our lives

All: We praise and thank you.

Catechist: For the promise of a new beginning which he is making to us.

All: We praise and thank you.

Catechist: For the many ways he has been with us from our birth.

All: We praise and thank you.

Catechist: For your determination to succeed in us.

All: We praise and thank you.

Then the Bible or Lectionary is passed to each individually for them to kiss the passage from Isaiah and pray: "May your word not return empty but succeed in what it was sent to do."

The Priest or Catechist sprinkles all with holy water and says the Blessing:

May the God of Abraham, Moses, David and Ruth be with us. May he continue to give us the water of life and satisfying food.

May he open our eyes to see him in our lives.

May he bless us with new hearts, with his mercy and love.

All: Amen.

A suitable hymn may be sung.

Imagine a little green man arriving from Mars in his space-craft.

HE'S NOT GREEN, HE'S **PINK**!

OK. Imagine a little **pink** man arriving from Mars in his spacecraft.

What sort of questions would you want to ask him?

ER,..LET'S SEE...WHAT'S THE WEATHER LIKE ON MARS? DO YOU ALL SPEAK THE SAME LANGUAGE? DO YOU HAVE BARS ON MARS?

Fine. Now let's ask our little pink Martian to answer your questions.

YER WHAT?

What a pity, he can't speak English. Never mind. If he **could** make himself understood he'd give us some inside information about life on Mars. For

the first time we'd have information we couldn't have got in any other way, right?

RIGHT!

'ERE! 'E'S SHOOTING OFF AGAIN

That's OK. We've finished with him now.

The point is that some people think Jesus was a bit like that Martian: they think he came from another world (heaven) to give us inside information about God and about what God wants us to do.

JESUS, YOU'RE MY SON. GO DOWN THERE AND TELL THEM ALL ABOUT ME. AND TELL THEM THEY'VE GOT TO BEHAVE THEMSELVES — OR ELSE!

This is NOT what Catholics believe about Jesus. Let's try and explain what they DO believe.

HOLD TIGHT, THIS COULD GET COMPLICATED

Catholics believe that Jesus was God. But they also believe he was **truly human.** He was God **and** man. In other words, he wasn't a heavenly visitor who came to earth **disguised** as a man.

And he wasn't a heavenly visitor who came to earth **pretending** to be a man. Jesus was truly human. He was born into this world. He had to learn to walk; he had to learn to read and write. He couldn't have told you that one day Columbus would discover America, and he'd have been just as amazed as anyone else in Palestine at that time if Concorde had flown over.

WHAT'S THAT?

So Jesus wasn't an alien visitor from some higher realm with inside information to hand on. He was one of **us**. And that's why his life is so significant. In Jesus God and humanity meet. Jesus shows us that God and mankind were meant for each other.

Jesus **shows** us God in the only way we can understand — in a human life. He doesn't hand out statements

about God. He himself makes God present to us.

It's as though God said:

What, then, does the life of Jesus **tell** us about God? If you read the Gospels certain things stand out. Jesus forgives sinners; he heals the sick; he is compassionate; he is patient; he restores people to life; finally he gives his own life in love.

So the God Jesus shows us is a forgiving God, a compassionate God, a God who heals, a patient God, a life-giving God and, above all, a loving God. If we believe in Jesus we can no longer think of God as a remote, authoritarian God-in-the-sky. This God disappears for ever...

Jesus shows us another face of God. His word for God is "Father". And his relationship with the God he calls Father is one of warmth, familiarity and love. So much so that Jesus can say...

This doesn't only change our image of **God**. It changes our image of **ourselves**. We are not miserable slaves of a mighty and ruthless king. We are children of a loving God who Jesus tells **us** to call "Father".

And what does it mean to be a child of God?

The life of Jesus answers that question too. He shows us how someone who is perfectly in tune with God lives. He is not fearful, timid or anxious. His relationship with God is a mature relationship. He is not divided within. He knows who he is, and he faces the demands life makes on him without dithering. He is true to the message of life he proclaims. In short, he shows us what it means to be fully human and fully alive. He is the perfect picture of a true human being.

So Jesus shows us two things:

So Jesus wasn't so much concerned with telling us what to **do**. He was much more concerned with showing us who we **are**. And his mission wasn't so much to make us more religious...

It was to make us more **alive**!

Alive in the way he himself was alive; secure in the knowledge that he was at one with the God he called "Father".

Catholics and Jesus
Step one: *Personal Story*

Spend 5 minutes looking at the cartoons on pages 89 & 90 from "How to Survive being married to a Catholic." Then on your own respond to the following

1. Which cartoon best describes the beliefs of most people you know?

2. How do we know Jesus wasn't an alien visitor from heaven?

3. What kind of God does Jesus show us?

In small groups share your responses. Then a leader records the findings in the large group.

Step two: *Scripture Story*

Listen to the story from John 1: 35 -42, which is the Gospel for the Second Sunday in Ordinary Time, Year B.

Step three: *Initial reactions to this Story*

- Which pictures or words do you remember?
- Who do you want to find out more about?
- Which parts of the story do you find confusing?

Step four: *Input*

Background

a) **John's Gospel** in many ways is the Gospel of the Elder. John is the perfect disciple who wishes to feed on solid food – content not simply to believe but to know. John's Gospel often follows a fairly fixed pattern: – Come – See – Believe – Know. Many questions throughout the Gospel follow from the great questions put in John 1:38.
- What do you seek?
- Where are you staying?
- Come and see.

This "see – believe – know" shape runs through the Gospel.

b) What is to be *known* is knowledge about Jesus
i) He is the Revelation of God
ii) The Father has sent him
iii) He is in the Father – the Father is in him
iv) Jesus is the most adequate revelation of God and is the place where God can be known in the most perfect way.
v) No one can come to the Father except by Jesus.
vi) Jesus is the way of pilgrimage to the Father. We must go through him – not through Jerusalem or Mt. Gerazim.

c) "Behold the lamb of God"
Note Isaiah 53:7. Also the story of the Passover Lamb in Exodus 12:1-13. The lamb is an image of release from slavery.

d) "We have found the Messiah"
Jesus is the anointed one – the one who will set us free. The Messiah – the Christ – is a title not a surname. The Messiah is the one who will bring in the new creation, the new people, new Covenant.

e) "Jesus looked at him"
Again throughout John's Gospel we read that Jesus "looked at", meaning "saw into the depths of and called out the real potential which was hidden".
"What happens when the 'Lamb of God', the Anointed One, looks at me?"

f) "Simon – you shall be called Peter."
Cephas – Rock. In John's Gospel the naming of Peter takes place at the beginning – in the other Gospels it takes place at Caesarea Philippi and becomes the turning point of the story of Jesus.
You shall become: can be understood either as from now you will be known as Cephas – Rock: *or* In time you will become the Cephas Rock – but you must struggle to become what you have been named.
Note the Story of Jacob and the Angel in Gen 32:22-32: "Your name shall no more be Jacob – but Israel", meaning you shall become Israel. This again involves the idea of the CALL to live what we are called to be.

g) This "event" in John's Gospel is not simply a description of one evening or night in the life of Jesus, Andrew and the Disciple – but is a description of how we are all invited to become disciples of Jesus: it is a life-long journey.

Exercises

1. Jot some responses down to the following questions. Then share in small groups.
- What was it about Jesus that attracted the disciples?
- How do Andrew and the other disciple find Jesus different from John the Baptist?
- What was happening in Andrew when Jesus looked at him? What in him was being called out?
- What happened as a result of Andrew's stay with Jesus?
- Can you see yourself as "the other disciple" in the story?

2. Role play the story in small groups. Give everyone a part to play: John the Baptist, Andrew, the other disciple, Jesus, Simon. Give time to get into your character. Then continue the conversation between the characters for five minutes. What happened?

3. As Simon was called to become Peter, what are the implications for you in being called to "become" – husband, wife, single person, widow, parent, worker, neighbour to far and near, son or daughter of God?

Step five: How do the stories touch each other?

Compare the findings from the cartoons about Jesus with those from the Gospel of John. Where are they similar and different?

Step six: The call to change

On your own reflect on what I have to do to let the God who is Jesus of Nazareth call me.

Step seven: Liturgy

This focuses on the blessing of each candidate, sponsor, catechist and priest.

Read the RITE, paragraphs 95-96.

Again highlight the Bible or Lectionary: if possible, a little differently from last week.

PRAYER God our Father, our hearts are always lonely until they find their home in you. Invite us again to come and see so that we find out where you are staying and become immersed in the new life you are offering us. We ask this through Christ our Lord. Amen.

Blessing of candidates by sponsors or catechists. Then all those remaining should receive a blessing from each other.

Bless each person individually. Invite the person to stand, put your right hand on their head and then pray this Blessing:

Name May you find whatever you seek in Jesus our Lord.
    May you stay with him in all your comings and goings.
    May he look you in the face and call you into a new future.

All Amen

The session may be concluded by singing a suitable hymn.

Sorry to disappoint you, but we'd better warn you right away that sin is a pretty boring subject.

Pardon?

All right, let's see if they do. Which of these two roads would you take to get the most fun?

THIS WAY FOR | THIS WAY FOR
Greed | Love
Envy | Truth
Hatred | Trust
Deceit Cruelty | Justice
Prejudice | Kindness
Revenge | Integrity
Selfishness | Fedelity
Injustice | Generosity
Exploitation | Honesty
Resentment | Respect
Lust | Firgiveness
Avarice | Gentleness
 | Compassion

...ER

Well?

Right. And that's one of the most important things to grasp about sin as Catholics understand it. **It is harmful to human beings.**

HEALTH WARNING
SINNING CAN SERIOUSLY DAMAGE YOUR-SELF

Well it **is**. But that's just another way of saying the same thing. Remember: God is on our side. So the laws he gives us are for our benefit — to stop us getting into a mess. Just look at some of them . . .

Thou shalt not kill
Thou shalt not steal
Thou shalt not commit adultery
Thou shalt not covet thy
  neighbour's goods
Thou shalt not bear false witness
  against thy neighbour

Commandments like these do not restrict our freedom. They stand like a **No Entry** sign on a road that leads to human misery.

In other words, the commandments are made for **our** sake. We're not made for the sake of the commandments.

Certainly not.

Good question. And not an easy one to answer. In fact it's impossible to answer completely. But here's a hint . . .

FIRST: Have you ever seen a dog in a dilemma?

Right. People, on the other hand, are faced with choices and decisions all the time.

94

But the choices we make aren't only concerned with trivial preferences. We also have the freedom to choose how we'll live our lives . . .

SHALL I BE A BRAIN SURGEON?

SHOULD I GET MARRIED?

SHOULD WE HAVE A BABY?

Choices like these are not easy to make. Our whole future happiness may depend on what we decide. And naturally, our happiness is very important to us. So we tend to choose what we think will make us happy. But we're not always very good at it. In the story, King Midas thought it would make **him** happy if everything he touched turned to gold. Then he kissed his daughter and . . .

PING!

I BLEW IT, DIDN'T I?

We've all got a bit of the King Midas in us. We tend to want to satisfy our immediate desires. We want instant happiness. And sometimes that **blinds** us to the consequences of our actions.

At other times we **can** see quite clearly that a particular choice will lead to harmful consequences — for ourselves and for other people. But we still go ahead and make the harmful choice.

I **KNOW** I'LL FEEL LOUSY TOMORROW. AND I **KNOW** I'LL BASH THE WIFE WHEN I GET HOME. BUT THE HELL WITH IT. I'M **STILL** GETTING DRUNK TONIGHT

Choices of this kind are impossible to explain. They are the result of a quirk in human nature that we all experience but are powerless to get rid of. To put it in Christian terms: we have to live with a "fallen" human nature.

OH, BLIMEY. YOU'RE NOT GOING TO COME ON WITH ADAM AND EVE AND THE APPLE?

Not if it bothers you. All we're trying to point out is that human beings have to live with inner conflict. We are **divided** selves.

We may not know **why** we are like that, or how we got like that, but we do know that's the way we **are**. We **are** capable of choosing to take that left fork, even though we know it's a road that leads to nowhere. And frequently we **do** take it . . .

Dead End   Open Road

YPF920

So sin, strictly speaking, is an irrational act. It separates us from the things we **really** want.

Sin **separates** us from the people we love because we can't be at one with them if we constantly hurt them or use them.

Sin **separates** us from ourselves because it destroys our sense of self-respect.

Sin **separates** us from life because it makes us closed-in and self-centred.

Sin **separates** us from God because he wants what's best for us and we've chosen what's worst for us.

O.K. SO SIN IS BAD NEWS. WELL WHAT CAN WE **DO** ABOUT IT?

There's no human answer to sin. But there **is** a divine answer. It's the answer Jesus gave to those who acknowledged their sinfulness.

YOUR SINS ARE FORGIVEN... YOUR FAITH HAS MADE YOU WHOLE.

God's readiness to forgive is the only possible answer to sin. Where sin separates, forgiveness re-unites. Forgiveness brings hope to the sinner, it restores his dignity, it assures him that he is accepted. Forgiveness enables him to live again — free from anxiety and guilt.

BUT WHAT IF I GO OFF ON THAT LEFT FORK AGAIN AND AGAIN?

Well, God is ready to **forgive** you again and again...and again...and again...and again...

Catholics and Sin
Step one: *Personal Story*

Spend five minutes looking at the cartoons on pages 94 & 95 from "How to survive being married to a Catholic."

Then on your own respond to the following:

1. Do you think people still see sin as largely "nudge – nudge, wink – wink"?

2. How does breaking God's law harm human beings?

3. What can help us as we make choices in our lives?

In small groups share your responses. Then a leader records the findings in the large group.

Step two: *Scripture Story*

Listen to the story from Mark 1:14-20 which is the Gospel for the Third Sunday in Ordinary Time, Year B.

Step three: *Initial reactions to this Story*

What is the main point of the Gospel incident?
Do you find it strange that Simon and Andrew follow?
What questions would you like to ask about this story?

Step four: *Input*

Background

a) **John** "arrested" = literally, "delivered up". The ministry of Jesus in Mark's Gospel is going to be a disconcerting one, arousing opposition in its starkness and covered always by the shadow of arrest, sentence and death.

b) **The Good News of God:**
The Time i.e. the Reign of God is NOW. The *Kingdom of God is*
● a time of sharing bread with the hungry
● a time of sharing homes with the homeless poor
● a time when captives are set free
● a time when the deaf hear, the blind see, the dead are raised up, the lame walk, and good news is proclaimed to the poor.
● a time when we realise we are our brothers'/sisters' keepers.
● a time when we hunger and thirst for justice and peace.
● a time when we pour ourselves out for the hungry and afflicted.
● a time of forgiveness – seventy times seventy.

c) Repent and Believe

"Repent" – literally, start walking in a new direction. Walk in the direction pointed at by the values of the Kingdom. It means to "change your ways", to take on the mind of God – the mind of Jesus – and not simply "say you're sorry". "Believe" means to live out of the act of Faith that this is a real possibility and not an impossible dream.

The test of being a disciple is whether one is willing to take the risk and believe that God's promises are possible.

d) **In the Bible** sin is seen both as individual and social – both personal and universal. The root cause of sin is identified as idolatry, i.e. believing in the illusion rather than the reality; becoming our own "gods" rather than acknowledging that we are creatures of the one God who is Father of all; believing that the reign of God – Kingdom values – are illusion and not reality.

The images of sin in the Bible are very concrete and may be helpful. Sin is:

To go astray	Isaiah 59:2
To miss the mark	Jeremiah 7:19
To be twisted	Isaiah 59:13-15
To carry a hump	Gen. 4:13
To err	Jer. 2:11-13
To rebel	Gen 3:4-5
To harden the heart	Isaiah 6:4-7
To close one's eyes to suffering	Amos 2:6-8
To be unmoved by the sorrow of others	Matthew 25:42-44
To walk by	Luke 10:29-37
To commit folly	2 Samuel 13:12

Sin is never seen simply as purely individualistic. It has always a social dimension and a tragic dimension – we are both the contributors to and the victims of the reality we name as sin.

e) **The call of the Disciples**

Immediacy – a sense of urgency – characterises the first half of the Gospel according to Mark. The call and the following immediately carry the idea of *repent*, leaving all – taking a new way of life.

Fisherman – a good occupation in the time of Jesus. Fish from the sea of Galilee were exported throughout the Roman Empire.

Leaving nets and hired servants – in our terms "employers" who were well off – not the popular picture of disciples who were "poor, ignorant, simple men".

● The starkness of the call and the response faces us with the question: what do I have to leave in order to follow Jesus and undergo repentance and change of direction in my life?

● Because of the starkness of the call and the immediacy of the response there is a real danger in domesticating the impact of Jesus – making it a comforting rather than a disconcerting encounter. For example, some prefer to hear the call as addressed to the "first bishops and priests" rather than addressed to all of us.

Exercises

1. Respond to the following questions individually and then share in small groups:

- What do you think life was like for Simon, Andrew, James, and John before they met Jesus?

- What promises did Jesus make about life with him in the future?

- What changes would the four disciples want to make in their lives as a result of being with Jesus?

- Are you hearing any good news in your life now?

- Is there a danger of making this into a nice story in which the disciples aren't really changed?

2. Pick out some of the important values of Jesus and their opposites. Where do you stand yourself? Add to the chart and notice where you stand – on your own, then in small groups.

VALUES OF JESUS	OPPOSITE VALUES IN THE WORLD	MY VALUES
1. Love everyone – especially outcasts	Be selective – love people like you	
2. Learn to depend on each other and God	Be self-sufficient	
3. Forgive seventy times	Give a just punishment	
4. People can really change	Leopard's can't change their spots	
5.		
6.		

Step five: How do the stories touch each other

Compare the findings from the cartoons about Sin to those from Mark's Gospel.

How does the Gospel Story take it much further?

Step six: The call to change

On your own, reflect on how you might be missing the mark or hardening your heart at this time in your life.

Step seven: Liturgy

Focus on the crucifix. Place it in a central position and surround it with candles and flowers. Begin by playing some quiet music.

Prayer

We live in a society which often lives contrary to Christian values – a world which puts possessions before people, success before justice, strength before depending on each other and upon God. We pray that the Spirit will fill us with God's power and rid us of fear, complacency and prejudice.

Renouncing false values and affirming God's ways

Priest/Catechist: Do you promise to make yourselves open to new influences and be willing to walk in new directions?

Catechumens and Group: We do

Priest/Catechist: Do you promise to try to love everyone and not just the people who love you?

Catechumens and Group: We do

Priest/Catechist: Do you promise to believe that you can really change, that tomorrow can be different from today?

Catechumens and Group: We do

The crucifix is then passed around the group for each person to kiss.

Final prayer

God our Father, bless these journeyers with the power of the Holy Spirit. Rid them of all false values and weakness and lead them gradually to trust more and more in your power which gathers us here. We ask you this through Jesus Christ, our Lord. Amen

The Liturgy may conclude with the singing of a suitable hymn.

People who know next to nothing about the Catholic Church **do** know **one** thing and that is that Catholics have to go to Mass on Sundays. When you're married to a Catholic your Sunday routine is inevitably going to be affected by your partner's weekly visit to Mass. In this section we'll try to explain **why** Sunday Mass is so important to Catholics.

But explaining it isn't as straightforward as it seems. Catholics themselves have various reasons for going to Mass — some good, some not so good. Let's start with a picture...

Jesus, your're my son. Go down there and tell them to worship me properly...or else.

Right! I'll found the Catholic Church to do the job.

Peter, you're the first Pope. Hand my message on. Tell them straight.

Yes, Lord. Leave it to me and my successors.

Right priests! Make sure everyone goes to Mass on Sundays.

O.K. BOSS!

You've got to go to Mass on Sundays. . . or else!

A job well done.

Until fairly recently this was the sort of picture many Catholics carried round at the back of their minds. They saw the Church as a link in a chain of command between God and mankind.

This picture led some Catholics to go to Mass on Sundays largely out of a sense of obligation and out of fear of God's wrath. Today most Catholics would agree that the above picture is grossly misleading. And it's misleading for three reasons:

> **1.** It makes God out to be a tyrant who is out to get you unless you kow-tow to him.
>
> **2.** It makes Jesus out to be God's henchman who came to tell us what to do.
>
> **3.** It makes the Church out to be an organisation set up by Jesus to make sure we do it.

If you've followed the earlier sections of this book you'll realise that none of these three statements is true. And none of them accurately represents the belief of Catholics today.

SEE ESPECIALLY SECTIONS TWO, THREE AND SIX

Nowadays the majority of Catholics have much more mature reasons for going to Mass than fear of God's anger. But that old picture does still have **some** influence and, occasionally you **will** come across Catholics who go to Mass just to "keep their slate clean"...

WELL THAT'S **ME** IN THE CLEAR FOR ANOTHER WEEK

ST RUDOLPH'S NOTICES

You'll also come across Catholics who go to Mass out of a sense of fear and foreboding. They think something terrible will happen to them during the week if they miss Mass on Sunday.

I'LL GET YOU, BAGLEY!

Much more frequently you'll come across Catholics who go to Mass because it would be awkward **not** to go. This is particularly true of some teenagers who go because the rest of the family goes, but given the choice they'd rather stay in bed.

COME ON!

But the majority of Catholics go to Mass on Sunday because they believe it is central to their lives as Christians. So let's look at what Catholics believe is happening when they go to Mass.

The first thing to say is that Catholics don't think of the Mass as a church service which they attend. The Mass is an **action.** It is something Catholics **do** together. They're not spectators **at it**; they're deeply involved **in it.**

At Mass they re-enact what Jesus did at the supper he had with his disciples on the night before he was crucified. Here's how the Gospel of Luke describes it:

> He took bread, and when he had given thanks he broke it and gave it to them, saying, "This is my body which is given for you. Do this in remembrance of me." And likewise the cup after supper, saying, "This cup which is poured out for you is the new covenant in my blood. . ."

The words of Jesus "Do this in remembrance of me" have been obeyed without interruption for nearly 2,000 years. Every time Catholics gather for Mass they know they are there to do what Jesus did. And they believe that in that action Jesus, who died on the cross and was raised to life three days later, is made present for them.

The Mass is a sacred action which has a depth of meaning impossible to put into words. That's one reason why Catholics never tire of the Mass. As they go to Mass over weeks and months and years they enter more deeply into its mystery and get a bit more insight into its significance and its meaning for their own lives.

So if you asked a number of Catholics what the Mass means to them you'd probably get a lot of **different** answers. Here are some of the things they might say...

Catholics and Sunday Mass
Step one: *Personal Story*

Spend five minutes looking at the cartoons on pages 100 & 101 from "How to survive being married to a Catholic." Then on your own respond to the following;

1. Do you know Catholics who go to Mass out of fear or 'to keep the slate clean'?

2. Which person do you most identify with in the pews?

3. Why do you think most Catholics go to Sunday Mass?

Step two: *Scripture Story*

Listen to the story from Mark 1:21-28 which is the Gospel for the Fourth Sunday in Ordinary Time, Year B.

Step three: *Initial reactions to this Story*

What strikes you most?
Do you find anything strange?

Step four: *Input*

Background

Shabbat (Sabbath)
a) To this day the Shabbat lies at the heart of the faith of the Jewish People. It is welcomed in as 'the New Bride of the Holy One' each Friday evening. It involves a time of excited preparation for the coming of God's presence among us – nothing is to interfere with that time of God and time with God. It would be hard to over-estimate the importance of the Shabbat for the Jewish people. It gives identity. It is the experience of God's presence among us. It reminds us that the first to be called "Holy" is a unit of time, not a place or even a person: cf. Gen 2:1-3. It is God's time which in the time of the Messiah will be shared by all peoples: cf. Isaiah 56:1-8. It is a remembrance of the Creation. All is in God's hands and we can join in the celebration of God's creation.

The Shabbat is the most important of all feasts: for all others the time of celebration can be calculated by the Rabbis and teachers. The Shabbat time is determined by God – the Holy One – and is built into the very essence of creation.

It is a time for remembering. There are two traditions:

i) Remembering the day of rest – creation –– time for God – the fullness of God's activity: cf. Exodus 20:8, "Remember the sabbath day and keep it holy. For six days you shall labour and do all your work, but the seventh day is a sabbath for the Lord your God...for the Lord has blessed the sabbath day and made it sacred."

ii) Remembering the story of the Exodus that we once were slaves and now are free: cf. Deut. 5:15. "Remember that you were a servant in the land of Egypt and the Lord your God brought you out from there with mighty hand and outstretched arm."

One tradition places the emphasis on the rest of God, the other on the setting free action of God. The strongest tradition in the time of Jesus was on the idea of 'Rest'. Thirty nine types of work were prohibited, e.g. anything that wasn't absolutely necessary for the preservation of life should be left undone – along with many rules which might seem to us rather pointless like prohibitions in clapping one's hands or lighting a fire. Nothing should interfere with the Holy Rest.

b) **The healing of the man with the unclean spirit**
Focus on the question of which tradition do we follow:
i) Not necessary – could be done tomorrow: i.e. work interferes with the time of Rest; almost blasphemy – cannot be work of God; interferes with Holy Time.
or
ii) Remembering Exodus – setting free: Shabbat is the time par excellence for unbinding people from whatever keeps them enslaved.

Jesus in essence is saying to the authorities: "you who claim to know the tradition and who claim to put God at the centre of all– you do not know what God is like – you are keeping God bound and not letting him be free".

c) **"Be quiet"**
Jesus will not have himself recognised as the Holy One of God simply as a miracle worker.
In Mark's Gospel we cannot really know who Jesus is until we can stand at the foot of the cross and say, "In truth this is the Son of God".

d) **"Amazement"**
Always points towards the graciousness of God working in unexpected ways.

e) **"With authority"**
This points to one of the great questions of the Gospels – who is this? What kind of teaching? Where does he come from?

The immediate question is which tradition is the more authentic – the Rest or the 'one who sets you free'; and which is the more uncomfortable?

f) For Christians the Shabbat has moved to the first day of the week.
The question is raised for us: How do we keep it holy?
What do we remember?

i) What Jesus did for us in the past.
or
ii) What Jesus calls us to do for a remembrance of him.

Is the Sunday a passive participation or an active call to mission?

● Can the Mass, for example, be seen as an invitation to the worship of God or as a call to make God present in our lives?

● Do the words of consecration,"This is my body which is given up for you", refer exclusively to the action of Jesus, past and present; or are they also a call to what we should be willing to do for one another and the wider world?

● Is it possible that the Mass can separate us from life rather than draw us more fully into life?

● Is there a danger of identifying 'keeping the Sabbath Holy' with simply 'going to Mass'?

Exercises

1) Tick, cross or question mark each of the boxes. Afterwards discuss your responses in pairs and then in the larger group.

	Sunday is a day to rest from the burdens of the week.
	Sunday is the day we spend time with the family.
	Sunday is a time for double pay.
	Going to Mass is the holiest thing we do on Sunday.
	Sunday is the day when we visit family and friends.
	Sunday Mass draws together the pieces of the previous week and helps me face the coming week.
	Sometimes Sunday Mass seems to have little connection with the rest of my life.

(Copy of this questionnaire for photocopying on page 106)

2) Select some of the following questions, think about them individually then share in small groups.

a) How do the people in the story from Mark keep the Sabbath day holy?

b) Why are the crowds astonished and surprised by Jesus' behaviour in the synagogue on the Sabbath?

c) Do we all have unclean spirits or is it a question of individual mental illness?

d) When we celebrate Mass how does Jesus "destroy" the "unclean spirits" within us?

e) Remember a time when going to Mass on Sunday made a deep impression on you.

f) Remember a time when Sunday was:
- a very special day
- just another 'work day'
- a lonely day

Step five: How do the stories touch each other?

Compare the findings from the cartoons about Jesus with those from the Gospel of Mark. How do Jesus, the possessed man and the crowds celebrate Sunday?

Step six: The call to change

On your own reflect on whether there is anything you would like to deepen about your celebration of Sunday and of Sunday Mass.

Step seven: Liturgy

This liturgy focuses on the blessing, breaking and sharing of some ordinary bread. A small quantity of salt is also needed.

Let us pray
God our Father, you are always bringing us out of slavery and into a new life of freedom and true love. You command us to remember your promise and your deliverance; to remember how you worked through Moses and in an even more wonderful way through Jesus. May we remember him now as we bless and break and share this bread in his name. We ask you this through the same Jesus Christ our Lord. Amen.

The bread is then broken, dipped in salt, passed around and eaten.

(Salt and bread are symbols of the bitterness of the journey and the strength and endurance needed for it).

Final prayer
Blessed are you Lord our God who brings forth bread from the earth. As we break this bread we thank you, our Father, for the life and knowledge of yourself which you have given us through Jesus. As this bread gave life to Jesus may it give strength to your people so that all may be gathered from the end of the earth into your kingdom. We ask you this through Christ our Lord. Amen.

A suitable hymn may then be sung.

Tick, cross or question mark each of the boxes. Afterwards discuss your responses in pairs and then in the larger group.

☐ Sunday is a day to rest from the burdens of the week.

☐ Sunday is the day we spend time with the family.

☐ Sunday is a time for double pay.

☐ Going to Mass is the holiest thing we do on Sunday.

☐ Sunday is the day when we visit family and friends.

☐ Sunday Mass draws together the pieces of the previous week and helps me face the coming week.

☐ Sometimes Sunday Mass seems to have little connection with the rest of my life.

This is the story of Fred. Fred was a quiet, gentle sort of person, with a nice wife called Sue and two lovely children.

But Fred had always been unsure of himself. When Sue had agreed to marry him he couldn't believe his luck. And even now, after six years of marriage, he felt deep down that he wasn't good enough for her. What made it worse was that all his friends were high-flyers — with better jobs, better cars, and better houses than Fred had. When he was with them he felt like a nonentity. Secretly he envied them their confidence and their success.

Then one day Fred met someone who offered him a new job.

> You've got potential, Fred. You could go far with our Company. You could be **Somebody**— a Top Executive.

Fred rather fancied himself as a Top Executive... So he said...

> I'll take it.

> At last I'll be **Somebody**.

Fred was determined to succeed in his new job, so he applied himself.

He worked hard...

He kept well in with the boss...

He stayed late in the office...

And he took work home at the week-ends...

Sue and the children saw less and less of him...

> Mummy, who's that strange man?

But when Sue tackled him about it Fred said:

> I've got to get ahead. I want to be **Somebody**. And I'm doing it all for you. You should be grateful.

So he went on applying himself. He got promotion. And that meant he had more work and more responsibility. So he worked even harder...
And he stayed even later at the office...
And he took loads more work home at week-ends...
And his family saw even less of him.

> Who was **that**?

When Sue complained he said:

> Think of the salary increase I've had. Soon we'll be able to move into a bigger house.

> But I like it **here**.

> A man in my position should be moving up-market. This dump is no longer in line with my status.

So they moved to a bigger house. Then they got a bigger car, which was also more in line with Fred's status. And a boat, because that was in line with his status too. But when the children said...

> Can you take us to the seaside and sail the boat, Daddy?

Fred always said...

> I'm too busy. I've got a lot of work to do.

So they never went out in the boat. But it was in the front drive for all to see.

Fred went on working very hard. But gradually the long hours and the need to meet targets began to take their toll. He began to get irritable and morose.

When Sue complained Fred said:

> CAN'T YOU STOP YOUR NAGGING, YOU OLD BAG!

Soon they were all very unhappy — especially Fred. Only the thought of being **Somebody** kept him going. And he worked harder and harder to achieve it. But the harder he worked the more irritable and unhappy he became. Even his friends noticed the deterioration. They advised him to take a nice long holiday. But Fred said:

> I can't. There's too much to do. I can't leave it.

So although he felt terrible all the time and although his wife and children hardly dared speak to him, he went grinding on. Until one day two things happened. Sue and the children walked out...

And Fred collapsed with a perforated ulcer. In his hospital bed Fred had time to think for the first time for years. And he thought...

> How did I get into this mess? I'm stuck in here, I've lost Sue and the kids, and I don't know what to do next. I might as well be dead.

But he **hadn't** lost Sue and the kids. When they heard he'd been rushed into hospital, they rushed round to see him.

> Fred...are you all right?

> No... I'm in a mess. I wanted to be **Somebody** and now I'm Nobody.

Then Sue said quietly...

> You're **Somebody** to us, Fred. You always have been and you always will be.

> Yes! You're our Dad!

This was news to Fred.

> You mean you don't mind if I'm not a Top Executive?

> Not in the least. I love **you**, Fred, not your position in the Company or your salary.

In that moment Fred's image of himself as a Top Executive went...

POP!

And for the first time in his life he realised it was OK just to be himself.

> I'm Fred!

When he came out of hospital Fred handed in his notice and took a much more modest job. It wasn't easy because it meant a big cut in his salary and it meant saying good-bye for ever to being a Top Executive. It also meant moving back to a smaller house and selling the posh car and the boat.

But before selling the boat Fred took Sue and the kids out for a sail in it.

THE END

Christians have a word for what happened to Fred: they call it "Redemption". To be redeemed means to be made whole; to be made truly and fully yourself. Fred's problem was that he couldn't accept himself for what he was. He felt inferior. So he tried to substitute another 'self' — one he thought he **could** accept: Fred the Top Executive But Fred wasn't cut out for that kind of life, and instead of bringing self-fulfilment it brought self-destruction. Yet in the midst of destruction Fred saw the light. Through the love of Sue and the children he learned to recognise and accept the true Fred. The Top Executive died, and Fred himself began to live.

Fred's story is everybody's story. Not in its details but in what it reveals. Very few people are completely whole. The vast majority are wounded in some way.

THERE AINT NUTHIN' WRONG WITH ME!

Nearly everyone lives with fears, anxieties, phobias which prevent them from being fully alive and fully themselves. Like Fred many people try to make up for it by substituting something else. Anything will do: booze, drugs, sex, betting, wealth, hard work, politics, religion... The thing itself may be harmless, or even good: but when it's used as a substitute for real living it can be lethal.

YOU'VE ONLY GOT TO LOOK AT MY FACE TO REALISE I'M A VERY INTEGRATED PERSON WITH NO HANG-UPS AT ALL

Many people go through their whole lives relying on substitutes. Others, like Fred, are more fortunate. Something happens which forces them to face reality. In Fred's case it was illness and the fear of losing his family. For other people it might be failure, disappointment, dissatisfaction, unhappiness or any one of a number of things.

It's a painful experience coming face to face with the fact that you've been going down a blind alley,

perhaps for years. But it's the first step on the road to recovery.

I'M GETTING OUT OF HERE

The second step is realising that you are accepted for what you are. Fred discovered that Sue loved him for himself, not for what he achieved. Through Sue's acceptance he learned to accept his own limitations. He wasn't a high-flyer and never could be. But that didn't matter, now that he knew he was valued for himself. For the first time he was able to live without anxiety. He was a new man.

YOU CAN SAY THAT AGAIN

Christians recognise a pattern in all this — a pattern of death and re-birth And they learn it from Jesus.

Jesus was the true and perfect man who lived his life fully and completely And he brought this fullness of life to the people he met. By his love, warmth and friendship he made broken people whole. Jesus treated no-one as a write-off. He deliberately mixed with the outcasts and sinners of society and at a word restored their dignity and self esteem. He enabled them to live again.

I HAVE COME THAT THEY MAY HAVE LIFE AND HAVE IT TO THE FULL

But there was a price to pay. The true man, the complete man stood as a challenge to the pious, the narrow-minded, the guardians of conventional religion. They resented him and they resisted him. Eventually they had him killed.

Yet his death was not failure but fulfilment. Not an end but a beginning. Jesus broke through the chains of death and rose to a new life — a life that death could never touch again. He lives that life now and he still offers it to the world — just as he offered it to the outcasts and sinners of Palestine.

How do we receive it? Well, our friend Fred received it when he discovered he could be himself. For there's nothing vague about the life Jesus offers. It doesn't mysteriously creep up on us, like a Scotch mist. We experience it whenever we're saved from the destructive elements in our lives and begin to see a new path stretching out before us.

Very often the agent of new life is another person. Their love releases us and gives us new hope.

You're **Somebody** to us, Fred. You always have been and you always will be.

Yes! You're our Dad!

This is the redeeming love of Jesus Christ at work in the world.

19
Catholics and Redemption
Step one: Personal Story

Spend five minutes looking at the cartoons on pages 107 – 109 from "How to survive being married to a Catholic". Then on your own respond to the following;

1. Does the story about Fred sound true to life? How?
2. How do Sue and the children rescue Fred?
3. Do people really change like Fred does?

In small groups share your responses. Then a leader records the findings in the large group.

Step two: Scripture Story

Listen to the story from Mark 1:29-39 which is the Gospel for the Fifth Sunday in Ordinary Time, Year B.

Step three: Initial reactions to this Story

What did you remember about Simon's mother-in-law?
What did Jesus do to her and the crowds?
Any questions about this story?

Step four: Input

Background

Note the use of the word "straightaway" and the sense of urgency.

The Gospel, Mark 1:29-39 is divided into *three parts.*

1. vv. 29-31
a) The Healing of Simon's mother-in-law. Note the verbs in this passage and their similarity to the action of Jesus in the Eucharist. He took, blessed, broke, gave. Here he comes, takes, lifts up – she serves. It is almost a description of the movement of the Eucharist.

b) In Jewish anthropology of the time of Jesus:

Life = going up
Death = going down

Sickness = Divided against oneself
the absence of God
unable to give thanks
to be brought low
into the pit

To be lifted up = To be redeemed
to be able to give thanks
 all songs of praise are sung as you go up
to Jerusalem
to be integrated
to become oneself

The lifting up of Simon's mother-in-law has the idea of redemption – "restored to family" and carries a lot more than simply "getting better".

She served them: carries with it the idea of ministry and Diaconate.

2. vv. 32-34
All gathered together: carries the idea of prayer – listening to word of God.

Healing means setting free: it is the action of the One who saves – unbinding. Cf. Story of Exodus – Slavery to Freedom.

Not permitted to speak: This is often referred to as the "Messsianic Secret": we cannot know who Jesus really is until at the foot of the cross. He will be recognised not as a miracle worker, not as a healer, needing the testimony of Demons – but "in truth this is the Son of God".

3. vv. 35-39
A lonely place: i.e. a desert place. This is the place where you speak to God and where God speaks to you. For Jesus, prayer is not a cosy chat but discovering the will of God: how to be life giving in every situation; how to live out the life of the one who sets you free.

Jesus in this passage is –
● The one whom we seek and find
● The one all are searching for
● The one with a mission to preach the good news
● The one who proclaims, "The Time is fulfilled. The Kingdom of God is at hand: Repent and believe the good news."

"That is why I came"
Came from where? In this story Jesus came from the wilderness and from the arrest of John the Baptiser...

19

Exercises

1. Reflect individually and then in groups on the following questions:
  a) When have you been "lifted up" by another person?
  b) Have people who have tried to be helpful always succeeded? What is the authentic quality of true help?
  c) Does it make sense to you that Jesus went to a lonely place to pray?

2. Complete the table – individually, then share in groups.

WHAT JESUS DOES TO SIMON'S MOTHER-IN-LAW	WHAT JESUS DOES TO THE CROWDS	WHAT JESUS DOES IN MY LIFE
1. When told he came	1. When they gathered he...	
2.	2.	
3.	3.	
What happens next	What happens next	Then what happens

3. How do you think people felt before and after they touched Jesus?

4. What makes Jesus want to move on?

Step five: How do the stories touch each other?

Compare the findings about Fred and Sue with those from Marks' Gospel. Are they similar or different?

Step six: The call to change

On your own reflect on how Jesus takes you by the hand and raises you up. How do you then serve?

Step seven: Liturgy

This liturgy is based on the Rite: Minor Exorcisms, paragraphs 90-94. Again focus on the crucifix - if possible one with the arms of Jesus in an inviting or welcoming gesture. (It might be even possible to paint/draw)

READ Mark 1:29-31

Prayer
God our Father, you give us Jesus who is always picking us up, raising us high, enabling us to begin again a life of deeper service. Give us the courage to let him approach us, to ask for healing, to let the warring parts of ourselves make peace with each other. Let us then reach out to the crowds so that they find in us whatever they are looking for. We ask this through Christ our Lord. Amen.

Each person then signs their neighbour on the forehead with the sign of the cross and says

"Name May the sign of Christ's cross raise you up to a life of deeper service."

The signing could be done with blessed oil.

Conclude by singing a suitable hymn, e.g. "Lay your hands."

Notes!

20

The Rite of Election
Step one

Talk to the group about the Rite which normally takes place in the Diocesan Cathedral. Consult the Rite, paragraphs 105-124.

Step two: Scripture Story

Explain that you will use the leper story from Mark 1:40 - 45 (which is the Gospel for the Sixth Sunday in Ordinary Time, Year B) as a way to understand what is happening at the Rite of Election.

Step three: Initial reactions to the Story

What is the story about? Is there anything you find strange or don't understand?

Step four: Input

Background: Mark 1:40-45

A. We look at the shape of the Story of the Leper.
- The leper comes to Jesus
- Jesus touches and heals him
- Jesus gives instructions to tell no-one but go to the Priests and Temple
- The healed Leper tells freely
- Jesus has to live outside in the country away from the towns – yet all come to him.

B. Leper: One who is unclean – forced to live outside the community – in the countryside. To be cut off from the community is to be cut off from God.
A strange idea for us – that you cannot get in touch with God unless you are joined to the community – cf. Leviticus 13:45-46

To touch a Leper is to become a leper

"I will. Be clean": This is similar to "Be calm"; and all was calm – Cf. Mark 4:39: and "Let there be", and so it was – Cf Genesis 1.

"Say Nothing": Again, Jesus cannot be fully recognised until at the foot of the cross.

"Show yourself to the Priest": This was in order to be received back into the community and to give thanks to God in the Temple. Cf. Leviticus 14:1-9

Talk freely: The message about Jesus cannot be stopped.

Jesus out in the country. Jesus has now become "the leper" living out of the towns yet all come to him. We are saved by the "outsider" who welcomes "outsiders" in and becomes one with them.

C. You might like to ponder these questions with regard to the Rite of Election.
1. What request do I make of Jesus and his Church?
2. How do I wish to be healed?
3. What will happen to me if I really allow Jesus to touch my life?
4. What price will I have to pay or what price am I willing to pay to become part of the community of the Church?
5. How will it affect my life?

Exercises

1. First complete the boxes. Then compare what happens in this story with what happens in the Rite of Election. What's similar and what's different?

WHAT THE LEPER DOES	WHAT JESUS DOES
1. came to Jesus	1. is moved with pity
2.	2.
3.	3.
4.	4.
What did the leper do afterwards?	What happened to Jesus?

RITE OF ELECTION

1. We come to the Cathedral — Our names are called.
2. We ask fuller admission — People who know us, catechists, sponsors, priests, friends and family testify that we are ready and worthy
3. We listen
4. We are prayed with and for
5. We sign the book
6. We go home to live in a new way

2. Who are the people who take the place of Jesus in my life?

3. Talk through the practicalities of the Rite of Election. What happens step by step?
- What do we have to do?
- What do the catechists, sponsors, priest, bishop do?

Step seven: *Liturgy*

This liturgy is based on the Rite of Anointing, paragraphs 98 - 102. It needs some scented oil which is tastefully displayed, surrounded by candles. Play some quiet music to begin.

Priest: Prayer for blessing the oil.

Lord God, protector of all who believe in you, bless this oil and give the wisdom and strength it signifies to all who are anointed with it in preparation for their baptism. Help them to approach you in confidence just as the leper did. Show them how you will, in the future, take their weakness into yourself and lead them to the joy of new birth in the family of your Church. We ask this through Christ our Lord. Amen.

The priest then anoints the hands of each catechumen and group member and says:

"Name we anoint you with the oil of salvation in the name of Christ our Saviour. May his touch strengthen you with his power, who lives and reigns for ever and ever. Amen.

Conclude by singing a suitable hymn.

Make notes here......ADAPT! ....
these materials!
They are not intended to be placed into inquirers
hands as they stand! Make your own handouts.
cut out, add....Read the Guidelines and the
background carefully — these are intended only
for your use. ADAPT!

"This is a time of more intense spiritual preparation, consisting more in interior reflection than in catechetical instruction, and is intended to purify the minds and hearts of the elect as they search their own consciences and do penance. This period is intended as well to enlighten the minds and hearts of the elect with a deeper knowledge of Christ the Saviour."

(Rite)

THE LENTEN PERIOD
(Period of Purification and Enlightenment)
On making distinctions between people

R.C.I.A. distinguishes very clearly between three categories of people:
1. Those adults who have not been baptised.
2. Those adults who have been baptised but are "uncatechized".
3. Those adults who are baptised and members of another Church.

The layout of the final text of the Rite of Christian Initiation of Adults (1987) is significant and instructive.

- Part I "The Christian Initiation of Adults" *(pages 14-148)* is for unbaptised adults.

- Part II "Rites for particular circumstances" contains special chapters on "preparing uncatechized adults for Confirmation and Eucharist,"*(pages 223-224)* and "Reception of Baptised Christians into the Full Communion of the Catholic Church" *(pages 225-236).*

Uncatechized adults are those who were baptised as infants but who neither received further formation nor the Sacraments of Confirmation and Eucharist. *"Their status differs from that of catechumens since, by baptism, they have already become members of the Church. Hence their conversion is based on the"baptism they have already received, the effects of which they must develop". (R.C.I.A. Par. 376)*

What does this mean in practice?
Catechesis for this group for the most part corresponds to that of the catechumens but account should be taken that these adults have a special status because they are already baptised. *(R.C.I.A.Par. 378)*

Baptised Christians are to receive "both doctrinal and spiritual preparation, adapted to *individual* pastoral requirements". *(R.C.I.A.Par. 391)*

The candidate should learn to deepen an inner adherence to the Church where he or she will find the fulness of their baptism. The Rite provides suggestions for reception within and outside of Mass and at the Easter Vigil.

The Spirit of this Period

"This is a period of more intense spiritual preparation, consisting more in interior reflection than in catechetical instruction, and is intended to purify the minds and hearts of the elect as they search their own consciences and do penance. This period is intended as well to enlighten the minds and hearts of the elect with a deeper knowledge of Christ the Saviour." *(R.C.I.A.Par. 126)*

This is a time more of spiritual recollection (**re-collecting** all that has happened) than catechesis. The elect should relax their searching and ponder the mystery that they are elect, that God has searched them out and chosen them. They are invited out into the wilderness with Jesus to be stripped, laid bare, and transformed. This is the time to go back to the personal stories of the inquiry period: to ponder them again; to see them with new eyes; to reinterpret them so that where we once thought of them as stories of our searching for God we now see them as stories of God searching for us.

Involved in the prayer of the parish

If this is a time when the heart is more emphasised than the head it is obvious that we should concentrate on personal and parish prayer life. Perhaps we could encourage the elect to take part in Ash Wednesday, in the Stations of the Cross and Benediction, in the Prayer group, the rosary, in the fasting and alms-giving which all the people of the parish are invited to practise.

The Scrutinies: Rites of Healing

These "are meant to uncover, then heal all that is weak, defective, or sinful in the hearts of the elect; to bring out, then strengthen all that is upright, strong and good." *(R.C.I.A.Par. 128)*

The scrutinies are the means by which our hearts of stone are replaced by hearts of flesh. Perhaps they could be better called "Rites of Healing" or "long, careful look at our lives." In these rites our personal demons (of inadequacy, possessiveness, helplessness, boredom, indifference, jealousy, etc.) are exorcised: we are set free! They are intended to take place on the 3rd, 4th and 5th Sundays of Lent but can also be celebrated on suitable weekdays for pastoral reasons.

The structure is the same for each:
1. Proclamation of the word
2. Silent prayer after the Gospel
3. Intercession for the Elect
4. Healing: exorcism of demons –
    a) president's prayer
    b) laying of hands on individual in silence
    c) president's prayer with extension of hands over all the congregation.

Suggestions for celebrating the Scrutinies *(RCIA Par:128-133)*

1. The elect and their godparents might compose the intercessory prayers out of the group's sharing on the way in which these stories convert and free them.

2. The Gospel stories for these Sundays could be read in different voices, maybe even from different parts of the church.

3. The Gospel stories could be dramatized.

4. *Visually* each Sunday a banner could be introduced that adds a portion of the rainbow (the sign of Noah's election) along with a symbol corresponding to the gospel story – pitcher of water, candle, tree of life, binding and unbinding.

5. On the 3rd Sunday the baptismal font might be placed prominently but empty on the sanctuary. The small fonts at the entrance doors might be emptied. On the 4th Sunday the elect might be presented with their candles for use at the Easter Vigil. On the 5th Sunday the elect could come forward to receive, not the Eucharist, but salt – the preservative which is also the pledge of eternal life.

These rites lay bare the human heart – of everyone, not just the elect. Conversion is always a possibility and an invitation. What Jesus did in the lives of the Samaritan woman, the man born blind, and Lazarus he *now* accomplishes in our lives through these rites. Trust them!

The Presentation of the Creed and the Lord's Prayer
(R.C.I.A.Par. 134-136)

The presentations take place during the weeks after the celebration of the scrutinies.

Here the Church entrusts the elect with the documents which are considered a summary of its faith and prayer from ancient times. The Creed could be presented on a weekday during the 3rd Week of Lent; the Lord's Prayer on a weekday during the 5th Week of Lent.

Again we need to be creative and adapt these rites for our own people.

Holy Saturday Morning

It is assumed that the elect will be participating in the ceremonies of Maundy Thursday and Good Friday. It seems to make sense to gather the elect and their godparents and catechists together on Holy Saturday morning: to *re-member* all that has already happened; to anticipate the night to come; to tidy up any practicalities about the Vigil.

Choosing a new name

Perhaps something could be made of the "Choosing a Baptismal Name" ceremony. *(R.C.I.A.Par. 187-189)* Make an effort to write a liturgy prayer including the names of all the people who have influenced us for the good and brought us to this day.

Try to combine with the "anointing with the oil of catechumens" (*R.C.I.A.Par. 190*) which celebrates the strength and encouragement this group and many others have given to our bodies and spirits. Be generous with the display and use of oil; it could be perfumed and the anointing done with special tenderness and reverence for our bodies and persons.

Is all this really possible?

No, it isn't! But it is possible to take up some of these suggestions this year, alter things next year and gradually build up so that whatever rites are celebrated speak to the elect and the parish community. It would be a *colossal mistake* to think that all these rites *had to be followed strictly*.

The RCIA Text commands us to
Adapt to the uniqueness and needs of each group and parish

The following materials are intended for the use of priests and catechists and not for catechumens. They contain themes for five sessions of the Lenten period, a method for each session, and some practical suggestions. They contain the scriptural and theological background which the minister can adapt to suit his own people.

Method and timing of each session

It is especially hard to devise something to touch our hearts. It is hard for us to get away from intellectual reflection and doctrinal input and to really believe they are not of primary importance during this period. So be extra choosy as you adapt these materials. Perhaps they are still a bit too intellectual and you might think of better ways to use these Gospel Stories. Trust your feelings.

STEP ONE: Reflection on the previous celebration.
Recap of the previous week.
Introduction of new story. 15 minutes

STEP TWO: Read the Gospel Story. 5 minutes

STEP THREE: Initial reactions. 15 minutes

STEP FOUR: Input on the background and movement of the Story. 10 minutes

STEP FIVE: Deeper reflections/exercises
Choose ONE or TWO of the exercises provided – *NOT* all
of them. 30 minutes

STEP SIX: Various forms of prayer 30 minutes

The value of *30 minutes prayer time* is especially emphasised. It is important not to allow other things to eat into this. Also emphasised is the need to *select one or two exercises and not them all!*

R.C.I.A and the Lectionary

The following themes for the sessions (Nos 21 – 24) of the Lenten Period follow Year A of the Lectionary. This is in accordance with the General Introduction to the Lectionary which states that because the Gospels of Year A "are of major importance in regard to Christian initiation, they may also be read in Year B and Year C, especially in places where there are catechumens". *(Par.97)*

Alternative Routes
for the Lenten Period

The suggested themes outlined in these Sessions are not intended to be comprehensive; nor is it possible to suggest themes that would include all aspects of the Christian life. There are many areas to be explored and these **"alternative routes"** are proposed, with some possible reading material, to remind readers of other significant themes and to help in the process of discovering the treasures of our Faith.

Lenten Exercises
Through Lent with Luke: Margaret Hebblethwaite, *(Bible Reading Fellowship)*
Living the Beatitudes: L'Arche Daybreak Community, *(St Anthony Messenger)*

Midlife Crises and Conversion
The Enneagram, a journey of self-discovery: Maria Beesing & others, *(Dimension)*

The Seven Circles of Prayer
Space, Silence, Seeing, Suffering, Touching, Listening, Face to face with God
The Seven Circles of Prayer (Video): Housetop, 39 Homer Street, London W1H 1HL
The Seven Circles of Prayer: J Wijngaards, *(McCrimmon)*
Living from Within: Philippa Craig, *(Grail)*
Tools for Meditation: De Rooy, *(Grail)*
Sadhana: A Way to God: Anthony de Mello, *(Doubleday Image)*
The Song of the Bird: Anthony de Mello, *(Doubleday Image)*

Prayers of a Catholic People
Sunday Missals
Prayer of the Church
The Stations of the Cross – numerous editions
Helps to pray the rosary
To Honour Mary *(Marialis Cultus)* Pope Paul VI

Spiritual Reading – Modern
Praying the Kingdom: Towards a Political Spirituality: Charles Elliot, *(DLT)*
Prayers of Life: Michel Quoist, *(Gill & MacMillan)*
Reaching Out: Henri Nouwen, *(Fount)*
God of Surprises: Gerard Hughes, *(Darton Longman Todd)*
Books on the Lives of the Saints

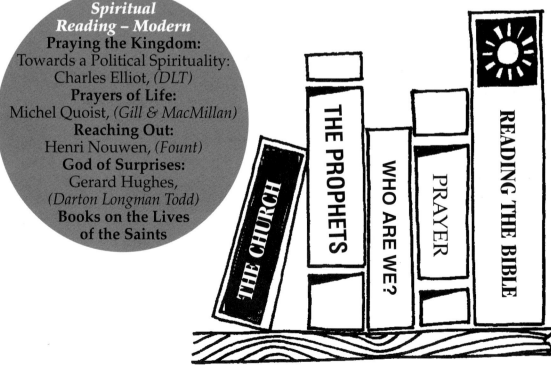

THE CHURCH
THE PROPHETS
WHO ARE WE?
PRAYER
READING THE BIBLE

The Testing of Jesus
Step one: Reflection

1. What do you most remember about the day of Election?

2. How did you feel on the way to the Cathedral and then going home?

3. What was it like:

- hearing your name called?
- meeting the Bishop?
- signing the book?
- seeing all the other people from different parishes?

4. What was it like to accompany the candidates from the position of catechists, Godparents or friends?

5. What was it like for any catechumens in the group who decided to wait longer rather than become one of the elect?

6. What was it like for catechumens who, because of marriage impediments, were unable to take a full part in the Rite?

Spend a few minutes reflecting on these questions and then share with the person next to you, and then with the whole group. Take 30 minutes for this reflection on the Rite.

Step two: The Scripture Story

Listen to the Story of the Testing of Jesus – Mark 1:12-15

Step three: Initial reactions to this Story

Take a moment of quiet to allow the story to speak, then invite everyone to share their immediate reactions in a word or sentence. Ask people to keep their comments very brief – more time will be given in Step Five.

- which pictures or words or actions do you remember?
- which part of the story strikes you most?

The secret of this step is to invite brief reactions not explanations. Write them on paper for all to see.

Step four: Input

Background – Mark 1:12-13

a) *The Spirit* is mentioned three times in the opening chapter of Mark's Gospel.
   i) "He will baptise with the Holy Spirit".
   ii) Heavens opened and the Spirit descends on him.
   iii) The Spirit drove him into the wilderness.

With the appearance of Jesus we enter into a new world – the power of God – the reign of God comes in a decisive way.

b) *"Drove him"* – a very strong word.

c) *Out into the wilderness* – a place of testing.
The possession of the Spirit and being the "beloved Son" does not spare Jesus from struggle and conflict.

The wilderness carries rich symbolic meaning in the Bible. It is where the great journey from slavery to freedom took place. In the Book of the Exodus, this journey takes forty years of wandering in the wilderness. It was then that the people murmured: "why bring us out to this wilderness to die? Who can feed us in this desert place"?

● A place of no security – no water – no bread – no meat.
● Better to live as a slave than pay the price of freedom.
● A place that reveals the heart of man/woman.
● A place of great danger – wild beasts.
● A place where it is easy to be lost and to wander in circles.
● A place where it is necessary to share and hold together.
● A place where it is necessary to know the way in order to get out.
● A place of refreshment – living water.
● A place where one speaks to God.

d) *Tempted* – a better word might be "tested".
During the forty years of the people wandering in the wilderness, they are found wanting.

● In Mark's Gospel, the desert twice tests the faith of the disciples who do not believe that God can provide bread in such a barren place.
   (Mk 6:30-43; 8:1-10)

● Jesus is tested and is found to be true. This testing of Jesus runs through the whole Gospel:
   in his conflict with the demons
   with his family and friends *(3:20-35)*
   with the scribes
   with Peter *(8:31-33)*
   on the cross *(15:33-39)*: "My God, my God why have you forsaken me"– but still "My God".

e) *Satan* = Prince of Evil: Prince of this world as opposed to the world of Jesus. The idea of Satan as tester or prosecutor of the court of God has a long history in the Bible, cf. Job chapters 1-2. The journey from this to seeing Satan as Devil – head of the dominion of evil bent on the destruction of people – is surrounded by uncertainty and has many pagan influences.

f) *Wild beasts:*
● Symbolic of the spirits of evil who inhabit the wilderness.
● A paradisiac image – it was held that in the garden Adam and the wild beasts lived in harmony. Here there is no apparent danger from them.
● For the one who has faith in God, who dwells in the shelter of the Most High – there is no danger. Cf Psalm 91.
● In the age to come when "there shall come forth a shoot from the stump of Jesse" *(Isaiah 11)* there will be harmony in all the world.Cf Isaiah 43:19-20, "The wild beasts will honour me".

g) *'The angels ministered to him'*
● In the Talmud one of the images of Adam in the garden was that he was waited on by angels.
● In Psalm 91: for the man of faith we are told, "He will give him angels charge over you".
● The prophet Elijah received the ministering of angels in 1Kings 19:5-8 during his forty days in the wilderness.
● Mark has no reference to Jesus fasting. We are doubtless to presume that the angels supplied Jesus with food; also that in the first struggle of the Gospel Jesus is not God-forsaken as he will be in the final struggle of the Gospel in Mk.15:34.
● The other people who are spoken of as ministering to Jesus in Mark's Gospel are the women who "looked on from afar" in chapter 15:40-41 and Simon's mother in law in chapter 1:29-31.

Background for Mark 1:14-15

Cf. Background notes on Catholics and Sin *(No 17 of the Formation Period)*.

Step five: Deeper reflections

1. Recall a time when you've felt tested. How did you feel pulled in different directions? What was for and against in making your decision? Did you go through a phase of "kidding" yourself about what was the right decision? Have you ever made a decision which went against the conventional wisdom but which you knew to be true?

OR

2. Jesus overcame his testings by faithfully depending on the Father. In hindsight can you see your coming through the times of testing as the action of God in your life? Who or what helped you get through it?

OR

3. (a) "Murmuring" is not just moaning but doubting God's power to change the situation. In this light think of the various ways people "murmur" today. Tell stories to illustrate.

PERSONAL MURMURS	SOCIAL MURMURS	CHURCH MURMURS
e.g. hurt, sickness	they bring it on themselves	we should concentrate on the next world and not this one
death, fatalism	get on your bike for a job the poor should pay their way	admission by strict rule keeping don't bother with them (non-Catholics, the lapsed, sinners) unless they conform

How do you answer these murmurs? How can we make them creative rather than being destructive and cynical?

OR

3. (b) MURMURING IN THE BIBLE
Work in pairs to look up these biblical stories. Choose different stories and then report back to the whole group. Notice how each story adds to and is enriched by the other stories.

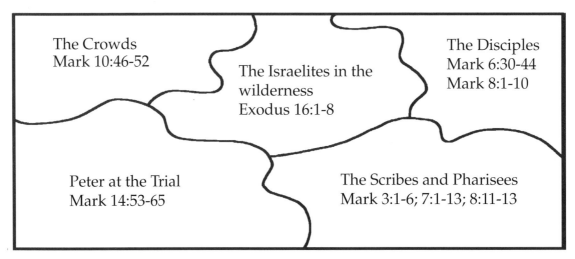

The Crowds
Mark 10:46-52

The Israelites in the wilderness
Exodus 16:1-8

The Disciples
Mark 6:30-44
Mark 8:1-10

Peter at the Trial
Mark 14:53-65

The Scribes and Pharisees
Mark 3:1-6; 7:1-13; 8:11-13

OR

4. TESTING IN THE LIFE OF JESUS

Work in pairs to look up one of the following stories. Then tell the stories to the whole group. Listen to how the jigsaw builds up. Do these stories show Jesus was 'tested' time and time again? Was it a genuine struggle for him? Where did he find the strength to overcome?

Mother, brothers, friends Mark 3:20-21;31-35	The Scribes Mark 3:22-27	Simon Peter Mark 8:27-33
In the garden Mark 14:32-42	The demons Mark 5:1-20	The Pharisees Mark 2:23-28 3:1-6
On the Cross Mark 15:33-39	A Pagan Woman Mark 7:24-30	Pilate Mark 15:1-3

To talk over with your Godparent/Sponsor

During the week spend some time with your sponsor/Godparent sharing your reflections and struggles on these stories.

Step six: Prayer

Here is a way of praying which, instead of making a big jump and starting with God up there, starts down here with our experience – with what is important to us, at this moment. It is only when we are really in touch with ourselves that we can see from God's point of view and ask him to guide our decisions.

So begin by relaxing, making ourselves comfortable. This is a personal way of praying – you won't be talking out loud or sharing it with anyone else, so relax and close your eyes. Think about what's testing you at the moment, what you're concerned about, worried about. What's your biggest concern at the moment? It may be work, family, your relationship with someone, or money, something else. (PAUSE).

Now how do you feel about it? Try to come into contact with your feelings about that concern. Worried? Frightened? Anxious? Hopeless? Lonely? (PAUSE).

Next we ask ourselves: Why? What makes it such a concern for you? What's behind it? What's at the root of it?

Think of a friend. Some good friend that you can trust. It may be your husband, your wife, your mother, a neighbour, some close friend. Got the person? Now in just a few words, try to imagine what advice that friend would give you about that concern? (PAUSE).

Now we have really got in touch with ourselves we are ready to turn to Jesus. Try to see Jesus' face. Notice how he looks when he is being tested. Notice how there's a struggle in him, how hard he finds it. Talk to him about your concern and listen to what he says to you about it. (PAUSE)

Now you're probably in a better position to know what to do about your concern. (PAUSE).

We end by asking God to bless us and our struggles, to strengthen us when we are tested – and not just for ourselves but for everyone here in the room. And now you can come out of your prayer; when you wish, open your eyes again and notice yourself and those around you.

It is often more relaxing if some very soft background music can be played during a meditation like this.

Make notes here..........adapt these materials! They are not intended to be placed into inquirers hands as they stand! Make your own handouts. – cut out. add ....Read the Guidelines and the background carefully – these are intended only for your use. ADAPT!

Jesus and the Samaritan Woman

Step one: *Reflection*

Recap last week's story and introduce the woman at the well.

Step two: *Scripture Story*

Read the text – John 4:4-42 – which is the Gospel for the 3rd Sunday of Lent, Year A. Arrange for the Story to be read in three voices: Narrator, the woman and Jesus.

Step three: *Initial reactions to this Story*

Use similar questions to Session 21.

Step four: *Input*

Background – John 4:4-42

a) **Samaritans** are the descendants of two groups – the remnant of the native Israelites who were not deported at the fall of the Northern Kingdom in 722 BC; and foreign colonists brought in by the Assyrian conquerors. Cf. 2 Kings 17:24. They were hated by the Jewish people.

b) Note the importance of "Well Stories" in the Bible. e.g.,
Rebekah meets the angel of God – Genesis 24:10-21
Jacob meets Rachel – Genesis 29:1-24
Moses and the daughters of the priest of Midian – Exodus 2:15-22

c) **The sixth hour**– literally 12 noon. Women only went to the well in the mornings and evenings, never at noon and never alone. Here the Samaritan woman coming alone and at noon points to the fact of her being an outsider even among her own people.

d) Jesus speaking to a woman and, more significantly, a Samaritan woman who was considered by Jewish People to be ritually unclean, would be very surprising and even shocking. The provocative nature of this meeting is very difficult for us to appreciate.

e) **The mountain** – Mount Gerizim is the Holy Mountain for the Samaritans; Jerusalem (particularly the Temple) is the Holy Mountain for the Jews. Jesus claims that the presence of God is now found in him – a remarkable claim. Cf. Story of ten lepers – Luke 17:11-19.

f) **Living Water** Cf. Stories of "wells" and the story of "Water from the Rocks" in Exodus 17. Again, it is very difficult for us to appreciate the significance of water for the people of the Near East, both then and now.

g) The Story of the Samaritan woman is one of the great encounters with Jesus. It reveals Jesus' true identity as one who can satisfy the deepest thirst of the human heart, the satisfaction of which John's Gospel calls "life".

The progression of the story shows Jesus revealing himself, and his identity, to the Samaritan woman. The story also shows the Samaritan woman growing in her insight into the true identity of Jesus.

Progressively, she identifies him as –
  i)   a Jew
  ii)   a prophet
  iii)   then she wonders whether he might be the long awaited Messiah.
  iv)   and finally she stands with the Samaritans in proclaiming him to be the saviour of the world.

Note the ways she keeps him at a distance and continually defends herself against him.
● "You are a Jew"

● "You have nothing to draw with"

● "the well is deep"

● "are you greater than Jacob?"

● "I have no husband"

h) **Samaritan Woman** Jesus' willingness to discuss theology with a woman, and even more so a Samaritan woman, should be noted. The dialogue between Jesus and the woman is of the greatest importance. As in all of John's Gospel the questions and answers operate at a number of levels.

The similarity between the stories of the call of Andrew and Simon in John chapter 1 and the Samaritans in this episode might also be worth noting.

● Come and see a man who told me all I ever did

● Can he be the Christ?

● Stay with us

● We believe because of your words

● We know "this is indeed the Saviour of the World"

Step five: Deeper reflections

1. a) Think of a time when someone asked for your help and you felt like this
woman – "Them (him, her) asking me!"
b) What did you do?
c) What difference did it make?
d) Did you ever change as a result of such a surprising request?
e) What price did you have to pay? How painful was it? What did you learn?

OR

2. a) Read the dialogue in the story and list what the woman says to keep Jesus at
a distance. Pick out the ways he leads her to a fuller understanding of who
he is.
b) Divide into pairs and choose to be either the woman or Jesus. Get yourself
into their shoes for a minute or two as you would very loosely imagine it.
Allow for natural resistence, embarrassment and awkwardness. Try initially
for just a couple of minutes. Perhaps catechists/priests could "demonstrate"
to the whole group before beginning in pairs?

In the large group afterwards encourage people to say what it was like for them.
Did it "come alive"? Did they learn anything?

OR

3. a) Imagine the woman talking to her "husband" a month afterwards. In pairs
be the characters and continue the conversation: e.g. the husband begins,
"What's wrong with you. You've been so different this past month...."
b) Imagine a similar conversation after a week between Peter and Jesus. In
pairs be the characters and continue the conversation: e.g. Peter begins,
"What really did happen with that Samaritan woman?...."

After both these exercises feedback to the large group. What was it like? What did
you learn?

OR

4. In asking the woman for a drink Jesus is saying, "I thirst for you", I need you.
How do you feel about Jesus telling you that he needs you now – comforted,
frightened, accepting, challenged?

Conclusion:

1. Whichever exercise you have chosen to do, link it up with your own personal
stories from the Inquiry Sessions.
- conversion
- treasure
- birth
- love
- death

2. Does the story of the Samaritan woman help you see more clearly, how God
acted in your personal story?

3. Can you identify a similar pattern between your own story and that of the Samaritan woman –
- invitation?
- rejection?
- acceptance?

To talk with your Godparent/sponsor

During the week spend some time with your sponsor/Godparent sharing your reflections and struggles on these stories.

Step six: Prayer

The Woman at the Well

> **Play suitable music to accompany this meditation.**
> **Do not rush it – allow time.**
>
> Begin by getting into a comfortable position.
> Take some deep breaths.
> Let go of any tensions – just relax.
> Imagine the Well.
> Notice the season of the year – notice the mountain.
> Feel the warmth or coolness of the air.
> See Jesus sitting there at the well,
> and imagine yourself sitting down beside him.
> Notice how you feel.
> Jesus says to you,
> "Give me a drink".
> How do you feel that Jesus is asking you for help?
> Look in to the depths of the well.
> Feel the coolness rising from the depths.
> And know that you are like the well.
> You have at your depth a well-spring of
> clear, cool water .....
> an unlimited source of wisdom...creativity...
> strength...goodness...power.
> Jesus recognises that you have the ability
> to draw up from your innermost depths...
> to bring to the light of your consciousness
> your own inner resources.
> Hear Jesus say to you,
> "If you knew the gift of God
> and who it is that is saying to you,
> Give me a drink, you would have asked him
> and he would have given you living water."
> Reply to Jesus and tell him

what your needs are now at this time.
Be peaceful and open to his love as he sits beside you.
Talk to him of your hopes, dreams, fears.
Hear him say to you,
"Whoever drinks this water
will get thirsty again;
but anyone who drinks the water that I shall give
will never be thirsty again:
the water that I shall give
will turn into a spring inside him;
welling up to eternal life."
Respond to Jesus –
Remember the words of the woman:
Sir, give me this water.....

(Finish by letting the music play softly and hold the
silence for as long as possible).

Make notes here.....ADAPT! ....these materials!
They are not intended to be placed into inquirers hands as they stand! Make your own handouts, -cut out, add...Read the Guidelines and the background carefully - these are intended only for your use.
ADAPT!

23

Jesus and the Blind Man

Step one: Reflection

Spend some time reflecting on last week.

Step two: Scripture Story

Read the Story – John Chapter 9. Arrange for the Story to be read in different voices: Narrator, Jesus, Blind Man, Pharisees, Parents and Disciples.

Step three: Initial reaction to Story

Use similar questions to Session 21.

Step four: Input

Background John 9:1-41

a) The Jewish Feast of Tabernacles is a feast which commemorates the wanderings of the people in the wilderness (Exodus) when they lived in huts or booths. Temporary huts covered with branches are set up to remind the people that they are dependent on God's protection. It is also a celebration of the bounties of nature.

In the ceremonies of Tabernacles during the time of Jesus there was a ritual lighting of the four Great Golden Candlesticks in the Court of the Women within the Temple area: when they were lit it was said that all Jerusalem reflected the light. The Temple literally became the light of Jerusalem. In the story Jesus claims to be the light not only of Jerusalem but of the world.

b) The many stories in the New Testament concerning blind people are worth noting: e.g. Bartimaeus *(Mark 10:46-52)*; the blind man at Bethsaida *(Mark 8:22-26)*; the two blind men of Jericho *(Matt. 20:29-34)*; the blind man of Jericho *(Luke 18:35-43)*.

Note, too, the sayings of Jesus concerning Blindness: e.g. "Tell John what you hear and see." *(Matt.11:4)* "Blessed are the eyes which see what you see." *(Luke 10:23)* "The eye is the lamp of the body." *(Matt.6:22-23)*

c) **Siloam** is the pool within the city walls which received the water "sent" from the spring of Gehon (gushing water) through the canal or tunnel built by King Hezekiah (c. 721 BC) as a protection against the Assyrian armies. The Spring of Gehon is associated with other stories, e.g. the capture of the city of Jerusalem by David in which the "blind and the lame" are attacked and hated. Cf 2 Samuel 5:6-10. (Note the new son of David who heals the blind and cures the lame.)

d) **"Who sinned?"** – It was popular belief that there was a direct causal relationship between sin and sickness and between righteousness and good fortune and health. Cf. also Luke 13:1-5; Mark 10:23-27

e) **"He made clay"** – possible symbol of the Creation of Adam *(Gen.2:7)*. Cf. also Job 4:19. Also possible reference to the Exodus story where the peoples' lives are made bitter with hard service in mortar and brick. Here in John the clay becomes a sign of blessing.

f) **"He does not keep the sabbath"**. Among the thirty nine works forbidden on the sabbath was kneading. Jesus has kneaded the dust with his spittle to make clay. The significance of keeping the sabbath is very difficult for us to understand, let alone feel. Cf. the background notes on Catholics and Sunday Mass No.18 from the Formation period.

g) **Put out of the Synagogue** – John's Gospel, written around the year 100 AD., follows the council of Jamnia 90AD at which there was the final break between the Jewish Faith and the Jew-Christians. At the council of Jamnia a sharp line was drawn between Judaism and the new teachings. The Jew-Christians were expelled from the synagogue. John's Gospel, chapter 9, refers to this painful dispute and not to the time of Jesus.

h) Note again the *dialogue* and the development within the story as the question is again asked – "who is this man?"

- "The man named Jesus"
- "He is a prophet"
- "Do you want to be his disciples?"
- "If he were not from God he could do nothing"
- "Lord, I believe, and he worshipped him"

Note also the contrast throughout the story between the "blind man" and those who claimed to see. Cf. Isaiah 6:9-13; Mark 4:12

"The Blind Man" "I do not know: one thing I know I was blind and now I see".

The others: "We know – and we can tell you he is not from God".

Spend some time on the contrasting dialogues within the story.

i) The Pharisees and the Jews in John's Gospel refer to those who oppose Jesus and are not to be understood as the whole people. After all, Jesus and his disciples were also Jews. Many Pharisees in reality were genuinely good people. They were shocked by the behaviour and claims of Jesus. He undermined customs of ritual cleanliness by his association with sinners. Many of his actions were seen as blasphemy.

23

Step five: Deeper reflections

1. **In small groups spend some time on the following questions.**
    a) Can you think of anyone you know who seems to you to be blind?
    b) What is it they are blind about?
    c) What happens when this is pointed out to them with care?
    d) How can "religious" people be blind about religion and about Jesus?

OR

2. For each of the following reflections re-read the conversation in the story.

Which of the characters in the story – the blind man, the Pharisees, the parents, the crowd – think that religion is a journey involving a constant change of mind and new beginnings; and which of them think religion is about arrival, about knowing the answers and not having to change any more.

Tick the statements below that seem to belong to "religion as journey" and cross those that seem close to "religion as knowing the answers".

	"Is not this the man who used to sit and beg?"
	Rabbi, who sinned, this man or his parents?
	This man cannot be from God; he does not keep the sabbath.
	How could a sinner produce signs like this?
	I only know that I was blind and now I can see.
	Do you want to become his disciples?
	Tell me who the Son of Man is so that I may believe in him.
	We are not blind, surely?

(Copy of this questionnaire for photocopying on page 140)

OR

3. a) Make a list of the ways in which the blind man changes his understanding of Jesus.
   b) Make a list of the Pharisees' hardness of heart (blindness) to the blind man.
   c) What is it in the Pharisees that even at the end of the story makes it impossible for them to "see"?

OR

138

4. a) Divide into pairs and choose to be either the blind man, the Pharisees, the parents or Jesus. Get yourself into their shoes for a minute or two to prepare and then have the conversation as you would very loosely imagine it. Try it for a couple of minutes only. Again catechists and priests could demonstrate to the whole group before beginning in pairs.

In the large group afterwards encourage people to say what it was like for them – did it come alive? Did they learn anything?

b) Imagine a similar conversation after a week between the blind man and his parents or between Simon the Pharisee and his friend Saul. In pairs be the characters and continue conversation, e.g. "You know I've realised now that it's not just about physically seeing but ...."; or , "Imagine him breaking the most important part of the law like that and still claiming to be a prophet...."

Again, feedback to the large group afterwards.

Conclusion

Whichever exercises you have chosen to do link it with the conversion stories of the inquiry period – perhaps the stories of treasures discovered later on in life.

- Blindness is common to us all
- For the blind man the recognition of his blindness is the very experience through which Jesus gives sight.
- Conversion is a journey which takes
  > time
  > patience
  characterised by
  > confusion
  > struggle
  > doubt
  > dawning awareness

Step six: Prayer
A meditation before the Blessed Sacrament

This could take place in the church – if it's heated – or in the room where the group meets. Decorate a table with cloth, candle, flowers. Sing a suitable hymn to begin and/or finish (e.g. Walk in the Light, The Light of Christ.)

Pray the meditation quite slowly with plenty of pauses.

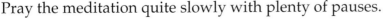

Lord, as we come before you we are aware of our blindness and ask you to make a paste and touch our eyes and help us really see. We come with all that's happened in our past, with the ways we've blamed you and others for what's gone wrong. We look and you remind us of the many times you have helped us to see – to see you, to see ourselves, to see each other, to see our world as you actually want us to be.

We are like the Pharisees: we want to box you in. We want to know who you are and where you are once and for all; we are afraid of letting you move! In searching for you we try to pin you down, to get things straight; but that can make us more crooked.

We try to imprison you in certain rules and certain people but forget that you are bigger than the sabbath and that you are alive in sinners as well as saints. We can also begin to feel that we are holy and so have nothing to learn. Take away our blindness, our hardness of heart, and give us new eyes and hearts of flesh.

When finding it hard to decide and difficult to choose, remind us of what you have already done and keep doing for us. Help us to share this good news with others who are searching that they, too, might walk in this new light.

So Lord, as I come before you in the Blessed Sacrament you ask me, "Do you believe in the Son of Man?" I reply, "Lord tell me who he is so that I may believe in him". "You are looking at him, he is speaking to you" is what you answer.

To talk over with your Godparents/sponsor

During the week spend some time with your sponsor/Godparent
sharing your reflections and struggles
on these stories.

Have a good week.

Tick the statements below that seem to belong to "religion as journey" and cross those that seem close to "religion as knowing the answers".

☐ "Is not this the man who used to sit and beg?"

☐ Rabbi, who sinned, this man or his parents?

☐ This man cannot be from God; he does not keep the sabbath.

☐ How could a sinner produce signs like this?

☐ I only know that I was blind and now I can see.

☐ Do you want to become his disciples?

☐ Tell me who the Son of Man is so that I may believe in him.

☐ We are not blind, surely?

24

Jesus and Lazarus

Step one: *Reflection*

Spend some time reflecting on last week.

Step two: *Scripture Story*

Read the Story – John Chapter 11. Arrange for the story to be read in different voices: Narrator, Jesus, Martha, Mary and Disciples.

Step three: *Initial reaction to Story*

Take a moment of quiet to allow the story to speak, then invite everyone to share their immediate reactions in a word or sentence. Ask people to keep their comments very brief – more time will be given in Step Five.

- which pictures or words or actions do you remember?
- which part of the story strikes you most?

The secret of this step is to invite brief reactions not explanations. Write them on paper for all to see.

Step four: *Input*

Background

(a) The event takes place in the context of the feast of the Dedication of the Temple and the Feast of Passover.

The Feast of Dedication commemorates the victory of Judas Maccabeus over the Syrians who had profaned the Temple by erecting their idol image on the altar – 167-164BC. After defeating the Syrians Judas Maccabeus built a new altar and re-dedicated the Temple. The Feast of Dedication was in a sense the feast of the re-birth of the Temple.

The Feast of Passover celebrated the great journey from slavery to freedom – death to life.

The story of Lazarus, whose name means, "God Helps", is obviously one of the key stories in the Gospel of John.

(b) Other stories help to throw light on the story of Lazarus. For example: Mary the one who *listens*. Martha distracted by much serving (diakonia).*(Luke 10:38-42)*

Anointing of Jesus. (*John 12:1-8*)
House of Simon the Leper. "What she had done will be told in memory of her." (*Mark 14:3-4*)
Parable of the Rich Man and Lazarus. (*Luke 16:19-31*)

(c) The story of Lazarus forms a trilogy of "un-binding" stories:

● The Unbinding of Isaac – Genesis 22

● The Unbinding of Lazarus – John 11

● The Unbinding of Jesus – John 20: 1-10

(d) Throughout the story, Jesus is always addressed as *Lord* by Martha and Mary – a post-resurrection title of Jesus.

(e) Note the irony and the faith dimension of the dialogues within the story. The questions and answers need to be addressed to all ages and to all who would seek a deeper knowledge of who Jesus is.

● **Disciples and Jesus** vv. 11-12

● **Martha and Jesus** vv. 21-22

● **Mary and Jesus** v. 32

● **Jews and Jesus** vv. 37-38

(f) Spend some time looking at the verbs used to describe Jesus and the actions of Jesus within the story.

(g) **"Jesus wept"**: shortest sentence in the Gospels. Jesus wept:
 i) because of his sympathy and love for Lazarus
 ii) because of their lack of faith – seeing death as final. Cf. John 14:1 and 14:27
    – "Let not your hearts be troubled; believe in God, believe also in me."

(h) "Jesus lifted up his eyes and said"
The prayer of Jesus is unusual in that it is not a prayer of petition as we might expect but a prayer of thanks giving (Eucharist). The same pattern of thanksgiving is followed in the "Priestly Prayer of Jesus" after the washing of the feet in chapter 13.

(i) "Cried with a loud voice" – an action that points to the power of God.
Lazarus, (= God helps) Come out (of the place of death)
There is a strong echo here of one of the great themes of John's Gospel: "I tell you most solemnly, whoever listens to my words, and believes in the one who sent me, has eternal life; without being brought to judgement he has passed from death to life." (*John 5:24*)

"Unbind him, let him go free" – Note the comparison with the direction given to Moses to go to the Pharoah and ask him to "unbind the people and let them go". (*Exodus 5:1f*) The story of Exodus and the God who sets us free runs through the story of Lazarus, along with the great question of Gen 18:14: "Is anything too hard for the Lord?" For example: "He opened the eyes of the blind man, could he not have prevented this man's death?"

The way these questions are answered calls us into real discipleship or rejection of what Jesus stood for:
"Many of the Jews who had come believed in him." *(v.45)*
OR
"From that day they were determined to kill him." *(v. 53)*

Step five: **Deeper Reflections**

Spend some time in small groups on one or two of the following questions.

1. Remember some of the stories in the Gospels which give us a sense of the feeling and deep humanity of Jesus.

OR

2. Look closely at the conversation between Martha and Jesus. *Read it again in two voices.*
Despite saying the opposite does Martha feel hopeless?
Was she right in not wanting to take the stone away?
What grounds did she have for hoping Jesus would keep his promise?

OR

3. Does Jesus raise Martha and Mary as well as Lazarus? Explain.

OR

4. What does it mean for Jesus "to cry in a loud voice,'Lazarus, here! Come out'."?

OR

5. What does Jesus mean when he says to the crowd, "Unbind him, let him go free"?

OR

6 (a) Divide into pairs and choose to be either Martha or Mary. Imagine you are talking to each other after the crucifixion of Jesus. Continue the conversation: "After everything that happened to us it never occurred to me that this would happen to him...."

6 (b) Divide into pairs and choose to be either Lazarus or the disciple Mark. Again imagine yourselves talking a month after the raising of Lazarus. Continue the conversation: "It's not just a question of living again but the difference is that now I'm free ...."

After either of these exercises feedback to the large group. What was it like? What did you learn?

Conclusions

Whichever exercise you have chosen to do link it up with your own conversion stories (of parenthood and social justice etc...) from the inquiry period.

- List the ways we seem to be dead/bound.
- Notice any ways you feel you've come alive or been freed.
- What areas of life continue to bind you?
- What does it mean for you to believe that God promises to raise you?

To talk to your Godparent/sponsor

During the week spend some time with your sponsor/Godparent sharing your reflections and struggles on these stories.

Step six: Prayer
A meditation on Lazarus

Again begin by relaxing and making yourself comfortable. We're not going to be talking out loud so relax and close your eyes. Feel your toes and let go of any tension there. Feel your feet and let go of any tension there, and so with your legs, your bottom, your stomach, your chest, your shoulders, your fingers, hands, arms, forehead, eyes, ears, cheeks and lips – let go and relax.

This time we're going to think about a concern I have for somebody else. One of the family – a friend – a neighbour – someone at work. We feel like Martha and Mary did for Lazarus. We feel like Jesus did for Lazarus.

Send for the Lord – tell him, "Lord the one you love is ill". He seems unconcerned, uninterested, deaf; we feel our last hope has gone. Then he starts to get involved but it is too late. What 's the point now? "If you had been here when we needed you my brother would never have died", we say to him. In fact we're disappointed and a bit angry with him: "Why didn't you come when you knew I needed you so desperately?" We think, somehow, that that promise he makes now seems empty and too late. It's all very well talking about heaven but I want something now. We become aware of our helplessness and deadness. It's not just my dear one who's aching, it's me too. In fact I'm just as dead as they are. There's no way out. A dead end.

24

We forget, Lord, that you are in great distress too; so much so that you weep with all your heart and still we don't notice. You know I never knew you loved me that much. I'm still afraid to roll the stone away. What will be unearthed for all to see? I know I'll have to change and that's so frightening. You seem to ignore my fears. "Lazarus, Martha, Mary, come out". You unbind us. You set us free. It's strange that whenever you free our brother and sister we feel different – it's not just them, Lord, it's me too.

It would be best to play soft background music and read the prayer slowly, with plenty of pauses.

Make notes here.....ADAPT! .... these materials! They are not intended to be placed into inquirers hands as they stand! Make your own handouts. cut out. add...Read the Guidelines and the background carefully – these are intended only for your use. ADAPT!

Preparation for Sacraments of Initiation at the Easter Vigil

The parish RCIA team will know which of their elect have already been baptised and which are seeking full communion with the Catholic Church. It is also essential for all group members to have the text of the Vigil Service for this Session.

A. An outline of the history and structure of the Easter Vigil

Explain the background and structure of the Vigil.

i) Background

The Jewish people have faithfully remembered their passover from death to life. They had been commanded that "it was a night of watching by the Lord, to bring them out of Egypt so this same night is a night of watching kept to the Lord by all the people of Israel throughout their generations". *(Exodus 12:42)* From the earliest times Christians devoted this night to watching and waiting for the Resurrection of Jesus. The Gospel of Luke is a reminder to have our lamps burning ready, to be like people awaiting our master's return, so that when he arrives he finds us wide awake and sits us at his table.

This night is the most important moment in the entire liturgical year. It is the time when we allow our Risen Lord to raise us out of the tombs of death, slavery and fear which we constantly inhabit. It is the time when we initiate newcomers into this new, dangerous way of living. They are the Sacraments of the dying and rising taking place in all of us. They are the symbols to be transformed which also transform us. *(Cf. Roman Missal Page 186-218)*

ii) Structure

The Vigil is arranged in four parts:

    a) a brief service of LIGHT

    b) LITURGY OF THE WORD

    c) LITURGY OF BAPTISM

    d) LITURGY OF THE EUCHARIST

Note that "it must always be borne in mind that the reading of the word of God is the fundamental element of the Easter Vigil."*(Roman Missal, page 202)* The most

25

important Reading is from Exodus 14, the Passover story, which was the central event in Jewish history, the first to be recorded for posterity and the story which moulds all the others. This reading should be highlighted in the Vigil Service.

What is proclaimed and heard in the Liturgy of the Word becomes visible in the use of the fire, light and darkness, in the pouring of water, the anointing with oil, the taking, breaking and sharing of the bread and wine. Obviously a cruet of water, a few sticks in the brassier, a thumb sized container of oil, last year's paschal candle, or bread and wine hidden on the sanctuary won't adequately express this new life which bursts out of the Risen Jesus and his people. If the symbols are to really change us they must be *abundant, prominent, fresh, beautiful and visible.*

Exercises
Taking the reading from Exodus 14 reflect in small groups on the following questions:

1. What makes this story so important for the Jewish people?

2. Thinking about the Vigil, how will *you* be set free from slavery?

3. Try to see the connections between Exodus 14 and any one of the other readings: e.g. Genesis – from chaos to order; Ezekiel – from heart of stone to heart of flesh.

4. Connect the symbols used in the Vigil with the stories of the testing of Jesus, the Blind Man, the Woman at the Well and Lazarus.
Questions, reactions – which symbol appeals most to you?

B. Rehearsal
Walk through the Vigil in the Church and outside where the fire will be. It is most important that the elect do not feel pressured into remembering what to do. Rather, this walk through the Rite should give them confidence to see that others will be there to guide them step by step.

C. Spontaneous Prayer
To acknowledge the group's hopes, fears and thanks.

Make notes here......ADAPT! .... these materials!

They are not intended to be placed into inquirers hands as they stand! Make your own handouts, cut out. add...Read the Guidelines and the background carefully – these are intended only for your use. ADAPT!

D *"This is a time when the neophytes are introduced into a fuller and more effective understanding of mysteries through the Gospel message they have learned and above all through their experience of the sacraments they have received. For they have truly been renewed in mind, tasted more deeply the sweetness of God's word, received the fellowship of the Holy Spirit, and grown to know the goodness of the Lord."* (Rite)

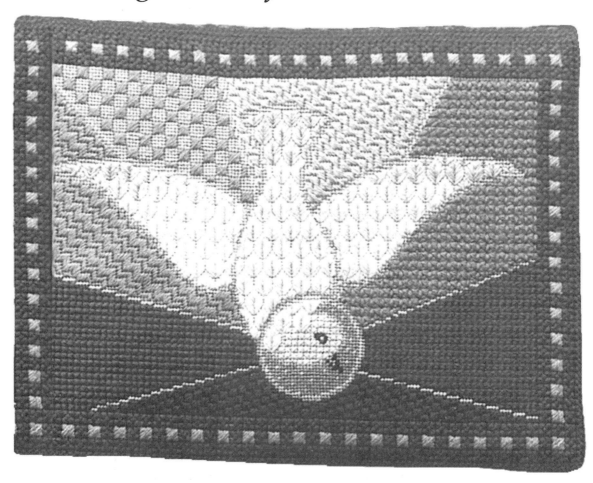

THE EASTER PERIOD
(Mystagogy)

The spirit of this period: post Baptismal Catechesis

"This is a time for the community and the neophytes together to grow in deepening their grasp of the paschal mystery and in making it part of their lives through:

- meditation on the Gospel
- sharing in the Eucharist
- and doing the works of charity." (R.C.I.A.Par. 234)

"The neophytes, with the help of their godparents, should experience a full and joyful welcome into the community and enter into *closer ties with the other faithful.* The faithful, in turn, should derive from it a renewal of inspiration and of outlook." *(R.C.I.A.Par 236)*

This period is every bit as important as the other periods which compose the total process of Christian Initiation. Once again, we keenly experience *the gap* between the R.C.I.A. vision and present pastoral practice. It is *not* the icing on the cake. Instead *it is the bread and wine, the basic food and drink of Christian life.* The new Catholics become apostles announcing to the Church and the world that there is something better than the promises of business as usual. They, who were once bearers of the promise, now become speakers of the promise.

The success of this period is in direct proportion to the depth of *our* conversion experience – has what preceded this Easter season been *for real?* Have we really died? If so, now we will truly rise to new Life.

1. Meditation on the Gospel

"The main setting (for postbaptismal catechesis) is the Sunday Masses for the Easter Season...These celebrations include particularly suitable readings from the Lectionary. *(R.C.I.A.Par. 237)*

It is significant that the main place for catechesis is *the Mass* and not the R.C.I.A. sessions. This underlines the fact that the new Catholics are a gift and a challenge to the whole parish community. How does their wonder, enthusiasm and freshness rub off on the rest of us?

In the early centuries candidates were not fully instructed about baptism, confirmation and eucharist until after they had received them. So the Sunday Gospel Readings, the Readings from the Acts, and the Second Readings from 1 Peter, 1 John and Revelation, should be used to help them reflect on *who they now are, what they are living for, where they are going* and *what gifts they have to give.*

Once again as a result of hearing the Scriptures the questions are:

- what did you hear?
- how do I become more convinced Jesus Christ is present to me even when I don't feel this presence?

The first Gospel story they hear is that of the empty tomb. There's no razzle dazzle, no promises for solving all personal problems. Instead emptiness of life yields a new lease of life, anxiety gives way to peace, preoccupations with self and one's own are taken over by a concern for everyone.

The basic message is not the simple answer of 'pop' religion – that everything will be alright till Jesus comes again. Instead we are given the sweaty challenge of renewing the face of the earth

- what does that mean in our homes, at work, in our neighbourhood and world?

Much is demanded of the preacher in this period and throughout the liturgical year. It might be possible for some of the new Catholics (or their godparents and catechists) to share something of "these happenings" with the whole parish at Mass.

2. Sharing in the Eucharist

"All the neophytes and their godparents should make an effort to take part in the Masses for the neophytes and the entire local community should be invited to participate in them. Special places in the congregation are to be reserved for the neophytes and their godparents." (R.C.I.A.Par 238)

If you go to Mass in a parish celebrating R.C.I.A. during Easter and do not know there are new Catholics in the parish then the parish doesn't know what it's doing with initiation! The new Catholics should be *visible* to the parish, and *part* of the whole Community.

It is important to attend carefully to the liturgical surrounds during the Easter season.

- Banners
- Posters
- Flowers
- Processional Cross with the white cloth
- and Easter Candle should all be prominent.

There can be a special blessing and sprinkling of the holy water reminding us all of our baptismal calling. Above all, robust liturgical signs are needed through which the message of new life is powerfully proclaimed.

3. Doing the works of charity

What are the new Catholics doing? What gifts can they offer? Christians are called and empowered to renew the face of the earth. The two most neglected and yet central ways this happens is through marriage and family life and through work. Married people have a vocation to make their home "a little church", "to bear witness to the love of God in the world so that the afflicted and the needy find in them generous friends". *(Solemn Blessing, Weddings)* Through work we are called to transform the world and be of service to all in our community.

Reflection and action on these two basic ministries is vital during this period. At the heart of our baptism is a call to mission, to ever deeper involvement in the world. Our new Catholics need encouragement to get involved with secular society as part of their ministry.

4. "Closer ties with the faithful"

This is obviously achieved through Sunday Mass but we need to look for more informal ways of making friendships and working together. Some of the parishioners might be invited to the group meeting to share their experiences of family life and work. Members of parish organisations could speak about their working for the Kingdom.

It might be possible to hold some house Masses and invite the Catholics of the surrounding neighbourhood.

"To close the period of postbaptismal catechesis, some sort of celebration should be held at the end of the Easter season near Pentecost Sunday." *(R.C.I.A.Par 239)*

This could vary from a parish barbecue to a Pentecost Vigil to celebrate liturgically the success of the past year and point to the work that remains to be done – now with more shoulders to carry the load.

Method and timing for each session

It is especially hard to devise something to touch our hearts. It is hard for us to get away from intellectual reflection and doctrinal input and to really believe they are not of primary importance during this period. So be extra choosy as you adapt these materials. Perhaps they are still a bit too intellectual and you might think of better ways to use these Gospel Stories. Trust your feelings.

STEP ONE: Reflection on the previous celebration.
Recap of the previous week.
Introduction of new story. 15 minutes

STEP TWO: Read the Gospel Story/Initial reactions. 5 minutes

STEP THREE: Input on the background and movement of the Story.
20 minutes

STEP FOUR: Deeper reflections/exercises
Choose ONE or TWO of the exercises provided – NOT all
of them. 30 minutes

STEP FIVE: Various forms of prayer 30 minutes

The value of 30 MINUTES PRAYER TIME is especially emphasised. It is important not to allow other things to eat into this. Also emphasised is the need to SELECT ONE OR TWO EXERCISES AND NOT THEM ALL!

R.C.I.A. and the Lectionary

The following themes for five sessions of the Easter Period follow Year B of the Lectionary. Alternative themes for Year A are also suggested from 3rd Sunday of Easter to 6th Sunday of Easter in Sessions 27A to 30A. As throughout the R.C.I.A. process it is important to adapt to the needs of the group and it should be remembered that these themes are suggestions only and are not intended to be used only as they stand.

The alternative themes (Sections 27A to 30A) require the use of "How to survive being married to a Catholic", published in the UK by Redemptorist Publications and in the USA by Liguori, available from the address on page 2.

Alternative Routes

for the Easter Period

The suggested themes outlined in these Sessions are not intended to be comprehensive; nor is it possible to suggest themes that would include all aspects of the Christian life. There are many areas to be explored and these **"alternative routes"** are proposed, with some possible reading material, to remind readers of other significant themes and to help in the process of discovering the treasures of our Faith.

The **Works of Charity**
Parish Organisations –
SVP, Justice & Peace Groups, Cafod, etc.
Neighbourhood Groups –
hospital visiting, baby sitting circles, toddlers groups, etc.
National Groups –
political parties, CAFOD, Trades Unions, Racial Equality, etc.

We celebrate the Presence of the Risen Christ in the Eucharist
We Celebrate the Eucharist:
Guidelines for Parents & Catechists, C Brusselmans
Together we Communicate:
Family & Resource Files: W Saris, *(Collins)*
The Book of SacramentalBasics:
Tad Guzie, *(Fowler Wright)*

The **Earliest Christians**
The Acts of the Apostles – New Testament
Refer to articles on Acts, 1 Peter, 1 John in New Jerome Biblical Commentary

Mary, Mother of the Church
Miryam of Nazareth:
Woman of Strength & Wisdom: Ann Johnson, *(Ave Maria)*
To Honour Mary
(Marialis Cultus) Pope Paul VI
The Mother of the Redeemer
(Redemptoris Mater) Pope John Paul II

26
Reflecting on Easter
Step one: *Reflection*

What was the most important thing that happened for you in the Easter Vigil ceremonies?

- How did the various symbols speak to you?
  Fire/darkness
  Paschal candle – light of the world
  Carrying the light of Christ
  Listening to the Word

  Call to renew Baptismal promises
  Entry into full communion
  Call to Baptism – Confirmation
  Clothing in a white garment
  Sharing fully in the Eucharist

- Being part of community in a new way

- Being called to live a new life

Step two: *Scripture Story*

Read the Gospel for the second Sunday of Easter, inviting the neophytes (now full members of the Church) to listen for echoes of their own experience of the Easter Vigil. The Gospel is John 20: 19-31

Step three: *Initial reactions to this Story*

Report back and record the initial reactions, keeping them as concrete as possible: e.g. first day, door closed, fear, filled with joy, receive the Holy Spirit, sins forgiven, "My Lord and My God". The input should be based on the responses to the story.

Step four: *Input*

Background

a) **First day of the week**
This is the story of a new creation – a new first day. Behind this story, and presumed by the writer, lies the accounts of Creation of the Book of Genesis, Chapters 1-3.

i) As the waters of chaos (Gen.1:1-2:4a) cannot stop God from bringing forth life, so the power of death cannot hold Jesus. Neither the sealed tomb nor the sealed room can hold back the power of Jesus. This Day is a new beginning, a new creation, a new way of life.

ii) Just as God breathed on the man Adam (Gen.2:4b-7) and he became a living being, so the Risen Jesus breathes on the disciples and they become a new creation, doing what Jesus did.

iii) In the account of Creation (Gen.1:1-2:4a), again and again we are told that "God saw that it was good" and in the creation of humankind that it was "very good" – original grace and blessing. In the new creation we read that the disciples are filled with joy on seeing Jesus. Jesus tells us that "Blessed (happy) are those who have not seen, yet believe". We all share in the blessing of the New Creation and not just those who experienced the original moment. True life is in believing and knowing that Jesus is the Christ, the Son of God. (John 5:24) Also refer back to notes on the story of the Blind Man in the Lenten Period, especially those on the Council of Yamnia. *(Session 23)*

b) "Peace be with you"
The first words of Jesus were "Peace", Shalom, be with you. The word 'Shalom' carries a great breadth of meaning. As well as being the ordinary means of greeting it carries the idea of wholeness, perfection, a state where nothing is lacking.

It involves the idea of being at one with oneself, one's neighbour and above all with God – literally in communion with God. It is a gift from God, a state of righteousness, and not mere prosperity and well being. Peace can be present in moments of great distress or difficulty. Peace, "Shalom" be with you, is like saying "The Lord be with you".

c) "His hands and his side"
The signs of the crucifixion are on the body of the Risen Christ, not taken away but changed to become signs of love, victory, forgiveness. Note the symbol of the Paschal candle with its five wounds of victory. We are called not simply to accept suffering but to transform its meaning.

d) "Receive the Holy Spirit" *(cf. Acts 2:4)*
In John's Gospel the gift of the Holy Spirit, the birth of the Church and its mission to continue the work of Jesus, is intimately and completely bound up with the Death and Resurrection of Jesus. There is no symbolic period of forty days.

e) Sins forgiven – sins retained
If we refuse to take away sin, to forgive, then sin continues to have power over us. Traditionally, this passage is seen as the power given to the Church to judge what sins can or cannot be forgiven. While this is true, it can also be seen as a statement of fact concerning the power of sin and the call to forgive which is present among the whole community of the Church and which needs to be

exercised by *all* members of the Church. This gift of forgiveness within the Church is celebrated sacramentally in the Sacrament of Reconciliation.

f) Thomas and his doubts

This highlights the difficulty of living in a world of faith rather than a 'rational world' that cannot cope with mystery and sees only problems. In the story Thomas functions as each one of us – "If only we had been there". But don't worry because, "Happy (blessed) are those who have not seen and yet believe". He also represents that 'uncertainty' often experienced before commitment to any serious decision in life – before marriage, commitment to single life, Religious or Priestly life, full communion in the Church, etc.

g) "My Lord and my God"

This spontaneous shout by Thomas is one of the great acts of faith in the New Testament. Thomas gives to Jesus the title given to God in one of the big stories of the Old Testament, the story of the Burning Bush *(Exodus 3)*: "Yahweh El... the Lord, the God of your Fathers". The title "My Lord and my God" was also one of the titles given to Roman Emperors during the period of the New Testament. John is reminding us that Jesus is the true Lord and Saviour of the world and that all political would-be saviours are false gods. This tension as to who is 'really' in control of our world continues to the present day.

Step five: Deeper reflection

Spend some time on one or two of the following exercises:

a) Has the input deepened or given any new insight into your initial reactions? Has it challenged, confirmed or raised new questions?

b) If this was the only story we had about the Risen Lord and his disciples, what would it tell us about the kind of Church, parish, family, etc. we should be?

c) On a wider level, is there a possibility of organising something like a Retreat afternoon to involve more of the Parish Community in reflecting on what it means to be a member of Christ's new creation, his Church, today?

Step six: Prayer

Decorate the Paschal Candle with flowers and position it prominently. Choose an appropriate hymn or music.

Take turns in praying a verse of the prayer
Adoro te devote

Godhead here in hiding, whom I do adore
Masked by these bare shadows, shape and nothing more.
See, Lord, at thy service low lies here a heart
Lost, all lost in wonder at the God thou art.

Seeing, touching, tasting are in thee deceived:
How says trusty hearing? that shall be believed;
What God's Son hath told me, take for truth I do;
Truth himself speaks truly, or there's nothing true.

On the cross thy Godhead made no sign to men;
Here thy very manhood steals from human ken;
Both are my confession, both are my belief,
And I pray the prayer of the dying thief.

I am not like Thomas, wounds I cannot see,
But can plainly call thee Lord and God as he:
This faith each day deeper be my holding of,
Daily make me harder hope and dearer love.

O thou our reminder of Christ crucified,
Living bread, the life of us for whom he died,
Lend this life to me then: feed and feast my mind,
There be thou the sweetness man was meant to find.

Jesu whom I look at shrouded here below,
I beseech thee send me what I thirst for so.
Some day to gaze on thee face to face in light
And be blest for ever with thy glory's sight.

Anon. XII Cent. - tr. G.M.Hopkins (1844-89)

Talk it over during the week with other people from your parish.

27

The call to witness

Step one: Reflection

Spend a little time helping the group to reflect on their experience of sharing in the Eucharist. The following questions might act as starters.

- As a result of sharing fully in the Eucharist over the past few weeks, what does it now mean in your life?

- How has your experience of the Eucharist changed as a result of entering fully into the Church?

- As a result of helping others to enter fully into the Church, what does the Eucharist now mean to you?

Step two: Scripture Story

Gather in the reflections and just record them without too much comment.
Listen to the Gospel for the 3rd Sunday of Easter, Year B – Luke 24:35-48. Then gather in the initial reactions of the group on any light that the Gospel casts on their original sharing. Again try to be as concrete as possible.

Step three: Input

a) The Eucharist celebrates the presence of the Risen Lord among us:
1) In the gathering, that is, coming together with a purpose – "Where two or three are gathered in my name..."

2) In the listening – to the Word of God, spoken and broken among us.

3) In responding – by thanksgiving.

4) In responding – by Communion.

5) In the missioning – "Go in peace to love and serve".

In the Eucharist we celebrate the Real Presence of the Risen Lord and we touch him through one another, through his Word, through the Eucharistic Prayer of the Church, through sharing in the consecrated bread and wine, through our being missioned to carry the Presence of Christ with us into the world of our daily lives and work. The Mass is 'now beginning'.

b) The shape of the Gospel, Luke 24:35-48, in many ways parallels the shape of the Eucharist.

1) The disciples gathered, sharing stories of what had happened to them on the road to Emmaus, meeting with the Risen Lord and recognising him.

2) Appearance and greeting – with a great mixture of reactions – terrified, startled, full of doubt, incredulous, overjoyed yet wondering.

3) Signs of the Real Presence of Jesus and not just a ghost – sharing a meal.

4) Instruction through an explanation of scripture.

5) A missioning – to preach to all nations. A going forth with good news.

c) "Peace be with you". cf. Notes on 2nd Sunday of Easter on Peace "Shalom".

d) "Look at my hands and my feet".
cf. Notes on 2nd Sunday of Easter on "His hands and his side", where the signs of hatred and rejection become the signs of love and acceptance.

e) "They stood dumbfounded".
Here is an echo of the two disciples on the road to Emmaus who "stood still, looking sad", unable to believe in the possibilities that were standing before them, and perhaps frightened of the consequences of belief.

f) "In the law of Moses, in the Prophets and in the Psalms".
The Jewish Bible, which we call the Old Testament and the Jewish community calls the Tanak, is divided into three: the Torah (first five books, the law of Moses); the Nebiim (the Prophets) and the Ketubim (the writings). The strongest argument that can be offered is one that is held together by the three cords of the Tanak. It is an argument which cannot be broken. The Psalms are part of the Ketubim. St Luke is saying that the whole of the Bible testifies to Jesus.

g) "That the Christ should suffer and rise from the dead".
There is no explicit passage in pre Christian Jewish Literature where one can find a mention of a Messiah who was to suffer or to rise from the dead. There are, of course, references to the Suffering Servant of Yahweh (cf. Is.53) and to the metaphoric coming back from the death of Exile to become a new people and the valley of Dry Bones, *(Ezekiel 37)* the life giving river that will flow from the Temple, giving life even to the salt sea *(Ezekiel 47)*. Also cf. references to the raising up of the Nation on the third day *(Hosea 6:2f)*.

h) "The third day" refers not to seventy two hours but to the day when God will act decisively.

i) "Christ would suffer and rise".
This is part of the original message of the early Church. The original credal formula is found in 1 Corinthians 15:3f: "I delivered to you .....what I also received, that Christ died for our sins.......that he was buried, that he was raised on the third day in accordance with the Scriptures and that he appeared...."

j) "Repentance for the forgiveness of sins".
The Good News is that we are reconciled and we are ambassadors of reconciliation to the whole world. St Luke's Gospel is the Gospel for and to the Gentiles: the birth of Jesus is Good News for all the world.

k) "Beginning from Jerusalem".
Luke's Gospel follows a simple pattern – the full Gospel includes the Acts of the Apostles. From Nazareth to Jerusalem; from Jerusalem to Rome, the centre of the non-Jewish world. The Acts of the Apostles ends with Paul preaching in Rome, i.e. symbolically the Gospel has reached to the ends of the earth.

l) "You are witnesses to this" – literally "of these things"; i.e. of the whole ministry of Jesus, cf. Acts 1:21 ff. What we have is not for ourselves but is to be shared. We are all ministers of the Gospel, of Good News.

Step four: Deeper reflection

a) In the light of the input, has any further light been thrown on your initial reactions to the story, Luke 24:35-48? Have they been affirmed or challenged? Have you discovered any new insights? Have any further questions been raised?

b) If this was the only story we had about the Risen Lord what, in the light of all our sharing, would it tell us about the kind of Church we should be and the kind of parish we should be?

c) On a wider level, perhaps it would be appropriate to organise a visit by the neophytes to other parish groups: e.g. Justice and Peace, St Vincent de Paul, etc. who are actively engaged in building up the parish and Church.

Step five: Prayer

Decorate the table and expose the Blessed Sacrament. Sing an appropriate hymn or play some music.

READ THE POEM – LOVE

    Love bade me welcome: yet my soul drew back,
     Guiltie of dust and sinne.
    But quick-ey'd Love, observing me grow slack
     From my first entrance in,
    Drew nearer to me, sweetly questioning,
     If I lack'd any thing.

    A guest, I answer'd, worthy to be here:
     Love said, you shall be he.
    I the unkinde, ungrateful? Ah my deare,
     I cannot look on thee.
    Love took my hand, and smiling did reply,
     Who made the eyes but I?

Truth Lord, but I have marr'd them: let my shame
  Go where it doth deserve.
And know you not, sayes Love, who bore the blame?
  My deare, then I will serve.
You must sit down, sayes Love, and taste my meat:
  So I did sit and eat.

George Herbert

PRAY THE PSALM
Psalm 15
Response: Show us, Lord, the path of life.

1. Preserve me, God, I take refuge in you.
I say to the Lord: "You are my God.
O Lord, it is you who are my portion and cup;
it is you yourself who are my prize." *Response*

2. I will bless the Lord who gives me counsel,
who even at night directs my heart.
I keep the Lord ever in my sight:
since he is at my right hand, I shall stand firm. *Response*

3. And so my heart rejoices, my soul is glad;
even my body shall rest in safety.
For you will not leave my soul among the dead,
nor let your beloved know decay. *Response*

4. You will show me the path of life,
the fullness of joy in your presence,
at your right hand happiness for ever. *Response*

Talk it over during the week with other Catholics

27a

The call to pray
Step one: Personal Story

Spend five minutes looking at the cartoons on pages 48/49 (Section 12) of "How to survive being married to a Catholic" (see page 154). In groups answer the following questions:

- Are these cartoons an accurate description of some of our childhood pictures of prayer and God?
- Is it true that many adults continue to pray like children?
- Does prayer as a relationship with God lead us to a more adult picture?

Step two: Scripture Story

Read Luke 24:13-35 which is the Gospel for 3rd Sunday of Easter, Cycle A.

Step three: Input

Background

a) **The Emmaus Journey** is not simply the story of a day but the story of the Journey to become a Disciple – a life long journey.

b) The shape of the story
- Two Disciples leave Jerusalem in despair. All hope gone, they go into exile. They discuss what had happened. What stories would they be sharing with one another?
- The Stranger, who walks with them, asks the question which forces them to share more deeply their shattered hopes with an outsider.
- The Stranger tells them stories out of their own tradition. What stories do you think he'd share with them?
- They have a meal and, in the blessing, breaking and sharing of the bread, they recognise the one who was with them all the time.
- They return to Jerusalem to tell the others.

c) The structure of the story is similar to that of the Mass.
   (i) Bringing our hopes and disappointments
   (ii) Listening to the stories of God's mercy (Readings and Gospel)
   (iii) Remembering what Jesus did and said
   (iv) Breaking and sharing of the food of life
   (v) Being sent to love and serve the Lord

(d) The irony within the story is quite strong:
   (i) Are you the only one who doesn't know what's been happening? – He is the one who does know.
   (ii) The women tell a story which amazed them but which is unbelieved. It might be worth spending time on the areas where we refuse to believe the truth because it comes from an 'unbelievable' source.

164

e) When they return they found the eleven "gathered together". This is the only time in the Resurrection stories where that expression is used – elsewhere they are just "there": "Gathered together" has the overtone of prayer – liturgy – "Where two or three are gathered together in my name I am with them".

f) What is it to have our "hearts burn within us" as he talks to us? Does this tell us something about the nature of prayer? i.e. listening to the Word of God – allowing it to speak to our deepest hopes and fears – and allowing it to bring about a change in our lives.

g) Note the fact that the two disciples are selective in their memory of the stories they share with one another. The stranger opens them to the fuller story of what "God's will" involves. There is always the possibility that each one of us can be selective too.

Step four: Deeper reflections

Spend some time in small groups on one or two of the following exercises:

A. Remember a time when you felt shattered and hopeless
   – who did you tell?
   – what did they say?
   – what happened?
   – did you find new hope?

B. Remember going to Mass when it made an impression on you
   – what hopes, disappointments did you take?
   – did the other people there help?
   – what do you remember of the scripture stories and homily?
   – what did you "offer" as your gift?
   – what was communion for you?
   – did you go home renewed?

C. Remember a time when you brought thanks / disappointments / requests to God in prayer
   – how did you feel?
   – how did you pray?
   – how did God speak to you?
   – did you hear anything unexpected or previously overlooked?

Step five: How do the stories touch each other?

What light does this gospel story throw on the cartoons?

27a

Step six: Prayer

Decorate the table and expose the Blessed Sacrament. Sing an appropriate hymn or play some music.

Read the poem – Love

Love bade me welcome: yet my soul drew back,
    Guiltie of dust and sinne.
But quick-ey'd Love, observing me grow slack
    From my first entrance in,
Drew nearer to me, sweetly questioning,
    If I lack'd any thing.

A guest, I answer'd, worthy to be here:
    Love said, you shall be he.
I the unkinde, ungrateful? Ah my deare,
    I cannot look on thee.
Love took my hand, and smiling did reply,
    Who made the eyes but I?

Truth Lord, but I have marr'd them: let my shame
    Go where it doth deserve.
And know you not, sayes Love, who bore the blame?
    My deare, then I will serve.
You must sit down, sayes Love, and taste my meat:
    So I did sit and eat.

George Herbert

PRAY THE PSALM

Psalm 15
Response: Show us, Lord, the path of life.

1. Preserve me, God, I take refuge in you.
I say to the Lord: "You are my God.
O Lord, it is you who are my portion and cup;
it is you yourself who are my prize." *Response*

2. I will bless the Lord who gives me counsel,
who even at night directs my heart.
I keep the Lord ever in my sight:
since he is at my right hand, I shall stand firm. *Response*

3. And so my heart rejoices, my soul is glad;
even my body shall rest in safety.
For you will not leave my soul among the dead,
nor let your beloved know decay. *Response*

4. You will show me the path of life,
the fullness of joy in your presence,
at your right hand happiness for ever. *Response*

The call to listen to the word

(Liturgy of the Word)

Step one: Reflection

This week focus on the Liturgy of the Word and how we listen to that Word. The following questions might help as starters.

- What do the readings of the Mass now mean for you?
- How do they affect your daily living?
- In what ways, if any, have they taken a new meaning?

Step two: Scripture Story

Gather in the reflections; again just record them without too much comment. Listen to the Reading for the 4th Sunday of Easter, Year B, – John 10:11-18. Then gather in and record the initial reactions of the group on any light or questions the Gospel throws on the experience of listening to the Word. Try to be as concrete as possible.

Step three: Input

Background

a) There is a great difference between sheep and shepherds here and in Israel. Here sheep wander free over hills and fields and are usually dogged into keeps. In the land of Israel even to this day the scene is quite different. The sheep flock together and follow the shepherd, who walks ahead: a striking visual image.

b) In the Old Testament, the king and the priests were often spoken of as the shepherds of the people – shepherds who neglect their flock (*cf. Ezek.34*). Due to this neglect the hope grew that God himself would act and become the true shepherd of his people. He would seek the lost, gather them into their true home, feed them with good grazing land, bring back the stray, bind the crippled, strengthen the weak and lead them in justice.

c) "I am the Good Shepherd."
A huge claim – taking on the prerogative of God. At the end of this passage we are told that there was a sharp division among the listeners.– i) He is possessed by a devil - out of his mind; ii) These are not the words of a demented person; surely a devil cannot open the eyes of the blind! – a reference to the healing of the blind man (*John 9*) during the feast of Tabernacles.

d) "Lays down his life."
The test of being a good shepherd is extended even to the point of death. The parable of the lost sheep pictures the trouble the shepherd will go to for a lost sheep. Here John extends the risk of the shepherd to death itself – a willingness to give one's life. Note also the reference to Jesus being "lifted up" throughout the Gospel, when he will draw all to himself. (*Cf. John 3:14; 8:28; 12:32*)

e) The hired hand and the wolf.
In the context of John's Gospel, the hired hand refers to the Pharisees who are in opposition to Jesus. The symbolism of the shepherd protecting his flock from wolves became traditional in the early Church. (cf. Acts 20:28-29 – Paul's advice to the elders of the Church at Ephesus.)

f) "Other sheep I have."
Verse 16 stresses that the purpose of knowing and being known is to bring the followers of Jesus into union with one another and with Jesus and his Father. The other sheep who do not belong to the fold introduces the idea of the mission to the Gentiles – the non-Jewish world. The whole question of the mission to the Gentiles was a real burning issue for the early Church. The Church only came gradually to understand the full significance of many of the sayings of Jesus: e.g. Matt 8:11, "Many will come from east and west and sit at table with Abraham, Isaac and Jacob in the kingdom of heaven".

g) "One flock – one shepherd."
Here the one flock – one shepherd refers to Jesus. He is the uniting force for the followers and not anything else. This has great implications for modern ecumenism.

h) "Laying down my life."
In John's Gospel the passion, death, resurrection and ascension form one action: cf. the image of the grain of wheat (*12:24f*). In the writings of John the image of the lamb slain (*Revelation 5:6f*) has much in common with the image of the shepherd who lays down his life, so that others may have life to the full. It might also be valuable to explore the image of the Suffering Servant of Isaiah 53.

Step four: Deeper reflection

Spend some time on one or two of the following exercises:

a) Has the input offered any new insights into your initial reactions? Has it challenged, confirmed, questioned, or raised further questions for you?

b) If this was the only story we had about Jesus, what would it tell us about the kind of person he was, the kind of parish/Church we should be?

c) On a wider level, is it possible to organise other groups within the parish to reflect on the Sunday Readings: if they already exist, to share in them, or to explore the possibility of a more ecumenical Gospel Reflective Group?

Step five: Prayer

Decorate the Paschal Candle with flowers and place it prominently. Sing an appropriate hymn or choose some music.

READ THE POEM

Glorificamus Te

I offer thee
Every flower that ever grew,
Every bird that ever flew,
Every wind that ever blew.   *Good God!*

Every thunder rolling,
Every church bell tolling,
Every leaf and sod.   *Laudamus Te!*

I offer thee
Every wave that ever moved,
Every heart that ever loved,
Thee, thy Father's Well-Beloved.   *Dear Lord!*

Every river dashing
Every lightening flashing
Like an angel's sword.   *Benedicimus Te!*

I offer thee
Every cloud that ever swept
O'er the skies, and broke and wept
In rain, and with the flowerets slept.   *My King!*

Each communicant praying,
Every angel staying
Before thy throne to sing.   *Adoramus Te!*

I offer thee
Every flake of virgin snow,
Every spring of earth below,
Every human joy and woe,   *My Love!*

O Lord! And all thy glorious
Self o'er death victorious,
Throned in heaven above.   *Glorificamus Te!*

An ancient Irish Prayer

28

PRAY THE PSALM

Psalm 22

Response: The Lord is my shepherd; there is nothing I shall want.

1. The Lord is my shepherd;
there is nothing I shall want.
Fresh and green are the pastures
where he gives me repose.
Near restful waters he leads me,
to revive my drooping spirit. *Response*

2. He guides me along the right path;
he is true to his name
If I should walk in the valley of darkness
no evil would I fear.
You are there with your crook and your staff;
with these you give me comfort. *Response*

3. You have prepared a banquet for me
in the sight of my foes.
My head you have anointed with oil;
my cup is overflowing. *Response*

4. Surely goodness and kindness shall follow me
all the days of my life.
In the Lord's own house shall I dwell
for ever and ever. *Response*

Talk to a friend about finding God in family life

The call to build the Church in your home
Step one: *Personal Story*

Spend five minutes looking at the cartoons on pages 44/45 (Section 11) of "How to survive being married to a Catholic" (see page 154). In groups answer the following questions:

- Which couple would you agree with?
- Are parents really their childrens' most important teachers?
- Do you pray at home? What more would you like to do?

Step two: *Scripture Story*

Read John 10:1-10 which is the Gospel for 4th Sunday of Easter, Cycle A.

Step three: *Input*

Background
(See also Background Notes for 28)

a) There is a great difference in the relationship between sheep and shepherds here and in Israel. Here sheep wander free over hills and fields and are usually dogged into keeps. In the world of Jesus, even to this day, it is common for the sheep to be individually named – they flocked together and follow the shepherd who walks ahead. A striking visual image.

b) Idea of the "watchman" from the Old Testament refers primarily to the prophet who protects the people from danger of any kind – a protection which often goes unheeded. cf. Jeremiah 6:17, Ezekiel 3:17, Isaiah 62:6.

c) In the Old Testament the King and the Priests were often spoken of as the Shepherds of the People – again sometimes as shepherds who neglect their flock. cf. Ezekiel 34. Behind these texts lies the truth that God is the real Shepherd who knows all by name, and suffers with them. This is the *call* for all who can be named as shepherds, e.g. Mother, father of a family – who have a role of caring for others.

d) Note the images Jesus uses of himself:
- I am the Door
- I am the Gatekeeper
- I am the Shepherd

How is Jesus the Door, Gatekeeper, Shepherd of each one of us?
How do we become the Door, Gatekeeper, Shepherd leading others to Jesus?

Step four: Deeper Reflection

Spend some time in small groups on one or two of the following exercises:

A. What's special about each of the members of your family?

B. Do you ever find yourself walking ahead of your husband or wife or your children? How does this make life harder for you?

C. In caring for your family how are you shepherding them?

D. Does your partner and your children shepherd you and each other?

E. How is the situation different if you are single, divorced, widowed or a one parent family?

Step five: How do the stories touch each other?

What light does this Gospel story shed on the cartoons?

Step six: Prayer

Decorate the Paschal Candle with flowers and place it prominently. Sing an appropriate hymn or choose some music. Ask the married and the widowed to touch their wedding rings as they pray.

READ THE POEM

Glorificamus Te

I offer thee
Every flower that ever grew,
Every bird that ever flew,
Every wind that ever blew.   *Good God!*

Every thunder rolling,
Every church bell tolling,
Every leaf and sod.   *Laudamus Te!*

I offer thee
Every wave that ever moved,
Every heart that ever loved,
Thee, thy Father's Well-Beloved.   *Dear Lord!*

Every river dashing
Every lightening flashing
Like an angel's sword.   *Benedicimus Te!*

I offer thee
Every cloud that ever swept
O'er the skies, and broke and wept
In rain, and with the flowerets slept.   *My King!*

Each communicant praying,
Every angel staying
Before thy throne to sing.   *Adoramus Te!*

I offer thee
Every flake of virgin snow,
Every spring of earth below,
Every human joy and woe,   *My Love!*

O Lord! And all thy glorious
Self o'er death victorious,
Throned in heaven above.   *Glorificamus Te!*

An ancient Irish Prayer

PRAY THE PSALM

Psalm 22

Response: The Lord is my shepherd; there is nothing I shall want.

1. The Lord is my shepherd;
there is nothing I shall want.
Fresh and green are the pastures
where he gives me repose.
Near restful waters he leads me,
to revive my drooping spirit. *Response*

2. He guides me along the right path;
he is true to his name
If I should walk in the valley of darkness
no evil would I fear.
You are there with your crook and your staff;
with these you give me comfort. *Response*

3. You have prepared a banquet for me
in the sight of my foes.
My head you have anointed with oil;
my cup is overflowing. *Response*

4. Surely goodness and kindness shall follow me
all the days of my life.
In the Lord's own house shall I dwell
for ever and ever. *Response*

The call to full life
(Liturgy of the Eucharist)

Step one: Reflection

This week try to focus on the Eucharistic Prayer and Communion.
The following questions might help as starters:

- What strikes you most about the Eucharistic Prayer of the Mass?

- What does receiving Communion mean to you now?

Step two: Reflection

Receive back the reactions, recording them without too much comment: e.g. "The night he was betrayed"; "This is my body"; "Do this in memory of me"; Remember the Church; May we all be one, etc. Try to be as concrete as possible.

Listen to the Reading for the 5th Sunday of Easter, Year B – John 15:1-8. Again gather in the initial reactions of the group on any light that the Gospel casts on their original sharing.

Step three: Input

Background

a) The setting in John's Gospel. The passage on the vine is part of the final discourse of Jesus, following the washing of the feet and the betrayal of Chapter 13.

b) "I am the true vine".
The image of the vine is very striking. Symbolically, the vine is Israel – Cf Psalm 80:9ff. Ezek.15:1ff.

- The vine is the wife, Psalm 128:3.
- The vine is the Royal House of Judah, Ezek 19:10ff.
- The vine is the image of luxuriant growth, Ezek.19:11ff. Hosea 10:1.
- The vine is the image of fertility. Psalm 128:3.
- The vine decorates the very Temple itself.

In the Old Testament Israel itself is seen as the vineyard, which is often depicted as unproductive and disappointing. (Jer.5:10; 12:10f.) Jesus making the statement, "I am the true vine", is taking to himself images from the Old Testament which refer to Israel, similar to, "I am the Way"; "I am the Good Shepherd"; "I am the Life".

c) "Every branch."
The meaning of the passage is clear. Just as Jesus is the source of life giving

water (*cf. Samaritan woman, John 4*) and is the bread from heaven (*John 6*), so he is the life giving vine. He is the one who makes us the People of God.

d) "Make your home in me."
It would be valuable to contrast this passage with the Eucharistic passage in John 6:51-58.

- The man who feeds on my flesh and drinks my blood remains in me and I in him.

- He who eats me will live because of me.

- I am the living bread.

These great metaphors need to be explored again and again, along with the metaphor of the vine and the branches.

e) "Whoever remains in me."
The true test of the disciple is to be in union with Jesus and what he stood for. The mission of the disciple is to bear fruit. Not even our union with Jesus is for ourselves.

f) Bearing and not bearing fruit.
Life is a committed life, i.e. knowing Jesus. A branch that does not bear fruit is not simply unproductive but dead. For John there are only living and dead branches, and even the living branches need pruning. Remember the setting in the Gospel – controversy, betrayal, washing of feet, understanding and lack of understanding. The passage refers more than likely to Christians who have 'converted' but are now dead. The language is similar to the imaginative words of Jeremiah to his own people: "Go through the rows of vines and destroy.... for they are not the Lord's." (*Jeremiah 5:10*) This is a harsh and difficult saying for us.

g) "You may ask what you will".
The requests made are to be seen in the light of the growth of Christian life, i.e. bearing fruit and becoming disciples. Communicating and sharing is the life of the disciple. Cf. John 8:31: "If you make my word your home you will indeed be my disciples, you will learn the truth and the truth will make you free." Cf also Matt.7:7-11; Luke 11:9-13; Mark 11:24: "Ask and you shall receive, seek and you will find...." In all cases, what we ask for and seek, is for the building up of the kingdom and living as true disciples.

Step four: Deeper reflections

a) In the light of the input, what new insights have you gained on your original responses? Have they been confirmed, challenged, opened up? Has the input raised any further questions?

b) If this was the only story we had about who Jesus is, what would it tell us about the kind of person he was/is, and the kind of parish, Church we ought to be?

c) On a wider level, would it be possible to organise a group/family meal (shared table) involving a sharing of what the Faith journey has meant for you. Talk about possibilities of offering the fruit we have received to others.

Step five: Prayer

It might be possible to focus on something visual - a banner, a poster, a journey motif. Sing an appropriate hymn or play some music.

READ THE POEM

Cantico del Sole (Canticle of the Sun)

> Most high Lord,
> Yours are the praises,
> The glory and the honours,
> And to you alone must be accorded
> All graciousness; and no man there is
> Who is worthy to name you.
> Be praised, O God, and be exalted,
> My Lord of all creatures,
> And in especial of the most high Sun
> Which is your creature, O Lord, that makes clear
> The day and illumines it,
> Whence by its fairness and its splendour
> It is become thy face;
> And of the white moon (be praised, O Lord)
> And of the wandering stars,
> Created by you in the heaven
> So brilliant and so fair.
> Praised be my Lord, by the flame
> Whereby night groweth illumined
> In the midst of its darkness,
> For it is resplendent,
> Is joyous, fair, eager; is mighty.
> Praised be my Lord, of the air,
> Of the winds, of the clear sky,
> And of the cloudy, praised
> Of all seasons whereby
> Live all these creatures
> Of lower order.
> Praised be my Lord
> By our sister the water,
> Element meetest for man,
> Humble and chaste in its clearness.
> Praised be the Lord by our mother
> The Earth that sustaineth,
> That feeds, that produceth

Multitudinous grasses
And flowers and fruitage.
Praised be my Lord, by those
Who grant pardons through his love,
Enduring their travail in patience
And their infirmity with joy of the spirit.
Praised be my Lord by death corporal
Whence escapes no one living.
Woe to those that die in mutual transgression
And blessed are they who shall
Find in death's hour thy grace that comes
From obedience to thy holy will,
Wherethrough they shall never see
The pain of the death eternal.
Praise and give grace to my Lord,
Be grateful and serve him
In humbleness e'en as ye are,
Praise him all creatures!

Francis of Assissi, trans. Ezra Pound

PRAY THE PSALM

Psalm 32

Response: May your love be upon us, O Lord,
as we place all our hope in you.

1. Ring out your joy to the Lord, O you just;
for praise is fitting for loyal hearts.
Give thanks to the Lord upon the harp,
with a ten-stringed lute sing him songs. *Response*

2. For the word of the Lord is faithful
and all his works to be trusted.
The Lord loves justice and right
and fills the earth with his love. *Response*

3. The Lord looks on those who revere him,
on those who hope in his love,
to rescue their souls from death,
to keep them alive in famine. *Response*

See if there are any parish or local action groups you would like to join – arrange continuing informal support

29a

The call to live and celebrate

Step one: *Personal Story*

Spend five minutes looking at the cartoons on pages 28/29 (Section 7) of "How to survive being married to a Catholic" (see page 154). In groups answer the following questions:

- Is it eye-opening to see the many ways we get in touch with each other?
- What are the different ways in which we say, "I love you"?
- Is it surprising to hear that Jesus continues to speak to us today through seven signs?

Step two: *Scripture Story*

Read John 14:1-12 which is the Gospel for 5th Sunday of Easter, Cycle A.

Step three: *Input*

Background

a) **The Gospel** is within the context of the Passover Meal: the Remembering of the journey from slavery to freedom. The whole story of Exodus is re-lived and told as our story – my story.

b) **"Do not let your hearts be troubled."**
Jesus has gone before us. Going before is one of the great images used to describe Jesus in the Gospels.
- Going before us to Jerusalem
  (rejection – passion – crucifixion)
- Going before us to Galilee
  (resurrection – new life – mission)
- Going before us to the Father
  (all in the hands of God)

How can we take more seriously that Jesus has gone before us – What difference does it or should it make to our lives?

c) **How can we know the WAY?**
The Way was the earliest description of the Church – we are people of the WAY.

I am the Way	I am the Door
I am the Truth	I am the Gatekeeper
I am the Life	I am the Shepherd

Again note the power of the images (metaphors).

d) "The Father and I are one."

Jesus is the greatest sign of God's presence in the world. He is the fullest expression of God in our world. To know, love and serve God is to know, love and serve Jesus. He is the sacrament of God for all of us. He is the sign of God in our world.

e) "He who believes in me will do the works that I do..."
- The disciple continues the work of Jesus.
- The Church is called to be the continuing sign of Jesus in the world – doing what Jesus did. cf. The statement of Jesus' mission. Luke 4:18-19.

Step four: Deeper reflections

Spend some time in small groups on one or two of the following exercises.
A. How has this group helped you on your way?
B. Will you miss it when it finishes shortly?
C. How can you continue to give and receive support from other people in the parish?
D. Do you intend to continue to serve informally or are there any groups you would like to join (in the parish, in the neighbourhood, in your town)?
E. How does all this connect with our Gospel story?

Step five: How do the stories touch each other?

What light does this Gospel story throw on the cartoons?

Step six: Prayer

It might be possible to focus on something visual – a banner, a poster, a journey motif. Sing an appropriate hymn or play some music.

READ THE POEM
Cantico del Sole (Canticle of the Sun)

> Most high Lord,
> Yours are the praises,
> The glory and the honours,
> And to you alone must be accorded
> All graciousness; and no man there is
> Who is worthy to name you.
> Be praised, O God, and be exalted,
> My Lord of all creatures,
> And in especial of the most high Sun

29a

Which is your creature, O Lord, that makes clear
The day and illumines it,
Whence by its fairness and its splendour
It is become thy face;
And of the white moon (be praised, O Lord)
And of the wandering stars,
Created by you in the heaven
So brilliant and so fair.
Praised be my Lord, by the flame
Whereby night groweth illumined
In the midst of its darkness,
For it is resplendent,
Is joyous, fair, eager; is mighty.
Praised be my Lord, of the air,
Of the winds, of the clear sky,
And of the cloudy, praised
Of all seasons whereby
Live all these creatures
Of lower order.
Praised be my Lord
By our sister the water,
Element meetest for man,
Humble and chaste in its clearness.
Praised be the Lord by our mother
The Earth that sustaineth,
That feeds, that produceth
Multitudinous grasses
And flowers and fruitage.
Praised be my Lord, by those
Who grant pardons through his love,
Enduring their travail in patience
And their infirmity with joy of the spirit.
Praised be my Lord by death corporal
Whence escapes no one living.
Woe to those that die in mutual transgression
And blessed are they who shall
Find in death's hour thy grace that comes
From obedience to thy holy will,
Wherethrough they shall never see
The pain of the death eternal.
Praise and give grace to my Lord,
Be grateful and serve him
In humbleness e'en as ye are,
Praise him all creatures!

Francis of Assissi, trans. Ezra Pound

PRAY THE PSALM

Psalm 32

Response: May your love be upon us, O Lord,
as we place all our hope in you.

1. Ring out your joy to the Lord, O you just;
for praise is fitting for loyal hearts.
Give thanks to the Lord upon the harp,
with a ten-stringed lute sing him songs. *Response*

2. For the word of the Lord is faithful
and all his works to be trusted.
The Lord loves justice and right
and fills the earth with his love. *Response*

3. The Lord looks on those who revere him,
on those who hope in his love,
to rescue their souls from death,
to keep them alive in famine. *Response*

See if there is any parish or local action group you would like to join – arrange continuing informal support

30

The call to mission
(The Rite of Dismissal)

Step one: Reflection

Focus on the Rite of Dismissal at Mass/Eucharist: "The Mass is ended. Go in peace, to love and serve the Lord". The following questions might help as starters.

- What does the final dismissal of the Mass :"The Mass is ended..." mean to you?
- How does the Mass continue to affect your daily life when you leave the church?

Step two: Scripture Story

After a few moments of silence, invite the members of the group to record their own findings on a piece of paper.

Read the Gospel for the 6th Sunday of Easter, Year B – John 15:9-17. Gather in the initial reactions of the group on any light that the Gospel casts on their answers. Record the initial reactions with little comment. Try to be as concrete as possible.

Step three: Input

Background

a) The Gospel is again from the final discourse of Jesus to his disciples, surrounded by washing of feet and the 'hour' which has come. The 'hour' is the time of testing – the time of the Passion and Death and Resurrection; the time when God acts decisively in the new life of Jesus; the time when Jesus draws all to himself; when he is lifted up. Note the double-edged sword of the imagery, Death/Resurrection, and the call to take on this way of life.

b) "As the Father has loved me."
Jesus is the image of God's love. To know God as Father we need to look at Jesus and what he stood for. For us to remain in his love we need to respond to his love as he responded to the Father's love. The opening verse points to a kind of 'Trinity' between the Father, Jesus and the disciples.

c) "If you keep my Commandments"
Love and obedience are mutually dependant. In the Jewish mind obedience carries with it the idea of being 'under the law' and therefore free, and so the obedience is a self-imposed way of life. To be 'outside the law' is to be lost, a wanderer, not knowing which way to go. We, as disciples, are 'under the law' of love. In John 14:31 Jesus says: "I do as the Father has commanded me so that

the world may know that I love the Father". In this sense "love, and do what you will".

d) "My joy – your joy"
The 'joy' of the Gospel comes from the experience of being loved and being loving. Without this joy Jesus would be unable to face the 'hour', and disciples would be unable to continue his mission and bear fruit. The theme of joy runs through the Gospel of John. From John the Baptist, whose joy is full on hearing the voice of the bridegroom (Jesus) *(John 3:29)*, to the Sower and Reaper who rejoiced to see the day of Jesus, to Jesus who rejoiced when Lazarus died so that the disciples might believe, to the disciples who were filled with joy when they saw the Lord, in John 20:20. The power of discipleship comes from this joy.

e) "Love one another".
A new commandment. The Tanak (Jewish Bible) is fulfilled in the two great commandments: "Love the Lord your God with all your heart..." and "love your neighbour as yourself". These are demanding enough. The commandment of Jesus that sets us free is to love as Jesus loved.

f) "Lay down one's life for one's friends."
The difference between what Jesus does and being willing to die for a cause lies in the fact that Jesus died to free all, even those who rejected him. Other passages in the New Testament which throw light on this call for the disciples to be willing to lay down their lives for their brothers and sisters are to be found especially in Matt. 5:44-45 and Luke 6:35-38. Also St Paul in Romans 5:7-8 reminds us that "It is not easy to die even for a good man...but what proves that God loves us is that Christ died for us while we were still sinners."

g) "I call you friends."
In the Old Testament, prophets often spoke of themselves as the servants of the Lord. In Luke 17:10 we are told that we are to say that "we are unworthy servants; we have only done what was our duty". In John, where the disciple has come to know and love the Lord, we are no longer a servant but a son. Perhaps the great parable of the Prodigal Son/Father *(Luke 15:11-32)* is echoed here:"I am no longer worthy to be called a son, treat me as a hired servant...Fetch the best robe and put it on him... My son, your brother was dead and has come to life".

h) "I choose you."
All is gift. We are all the elect; we are all appointed; we are all sent out; we are all commissioned. We are commissioned to bring the love of Jesus to others, to make disciples. To work for Justice and Peace is to bring forgiveness, to forgive sin, to love enemies, to bring about a change of heart, "to take the heart of stone and give a heart of flesh", to love one another. Perhaps one of the ways of exploring this Gospel is to spend some time pondering on the ways we domesticate and water down the power of this call.

Step four: Deeper reflections

Spend some time on one or two of the following exercises:

a) Has the input confirmed your initial reactions on the ending/beginning of the Mass? Has it challenged, given new insight, raised further questions for you?

b) If this was the only story we had about Jesus the Lord and his disciples, what would it tell us about the kind of Church, parish, followers we should be?

c) On a wider level, is it possible to spend time arranging a special parish event/liturgy to celebrate Pentecost, the birth of the Mission of the Church, within the parish?

Step five: Prayer

Decorate the table and expose the Blessed Sacrament. Sing an appropriate hymn or choose some music.

READ THE POEM

The Face of Christ

The tragic beauty of the face of Christ
shines in the face of man;
the abandoned old live on
in shabby rooms, far from inner comfort.
Outside , in the street
din and purpose, the world like a fiery animal
reined in by youth. Within
a pallid tiring heart
shuffles about it's dwelling.

Nothing, or so little, come of life's promise.
Out of broken men, despised minds
what does one make –
a roadside show, a graveyard of the heart?

The Christian God reproves
faithless ranting minds
crushing like upper and lower stones
all life between;
Christ, fowler of street and hedgerow
of cripples and the distempered old
– eyes blind as woodknots,
tongues tight as immigrants –

takes in His gospel net
all the hue and cry of existence.

Heaven, of such imperfection,
wary, ravaged, wild?

Yes. Compel them in.

Daniel Berrigan

PRAY THE PRAYER OF ST FRANCIS

Lord, make me an instrument of your peace;
Where there is hatred, let me sow love;
Where there is injury, pardon;
Where there is discord, union;
Where there is doubt, faith;
Where there is despair, hope;
Where there is darkness, light;
Where there is sadness, joy.
For thy mercy and truth's sake:
O Divine Master, grant that I may not so much seek
To be consoled as to console,
To be understood as to understand,
To be loved as to love,
for
It is in giving that we receive,
It is in pardoning that we are pardoned,
It is in dying that we are born to eternal life.

Bless each person individually

NAME May the Lord bless you and keep you.
May his face shine upon you and be gracious to you.
May he look upon you with kindness and give you his peace.
May almighty God bless you,
the Father, the Son and the Holy Spirit.

30a

The call to change the world

Step one: *Personal Story*

Spend five minutes looking at the cartoons on pages 52-54 (Section 13) of "How to survive being married to a Catholic" (see page 154). In groups answer the following questions:

- What effect does Fred's Catholic Faith have on his life?
- How could his non-Catholic wife have "saved him"?

Step two: *Scripture Story*

Read John 14:15-21 which is the Gospel for 6th Sunday of Easter, Cycle A.

Step three: *Input*

Background

a) **The wider context is similar to Session 29A.**

b) **"If you love me"**
In the Old Testament and New Testament the call to love God is very frequent. Usually, we are invited to believe in Jesus: the fact that now we are invited to love Jesus points to a further development of the truth that "the Father and I are one". We are involved both as a community and as individuals at the deepest possible level with both the Father and Jesus.

c) **The Spirit of Truth**
Note again all the images Jesus uses to describe himself over the past few weeks – Door, Gatekeeper, Shepherd, Way, Truth, Life...
The Spirit of Truth is the Spirit of Jesus and the Father who continue to live in the Church. The Spirit:

    i) Brings together the far flung peoples into one nation. Cf Acts 2

    ii) Unites the peoples divided by different languages. (Cf Tower of Babel as the occasion for different languages – Genesis 11:1-9) But now "we all hear each in his own language, the wonderful works of God".

    iii) Forms the Church as a people with a mission for all peoples.

Note: One of the great images of the Jewish People is that in the fullness of time – the time of the Messiah – all peoples will flock to Jerusalem, the holy mountain. The Christian development is not that all peoples will flock to us but that we are to go out and make disciples of Jesus: because "as the Father sent me so I send you".

d)"The world can never receive since it neither sees nor knows him."
In the Gospel of Luke this is expressed in the words, "he will be a sign of contradiction". Why? Because he will turn the values of the world upside down. Cf Luke 6 – Sermon on the Plain and Matthew 5-7 – Sermon on the Mount.
Ponder what would be the implications for us, our Church, our world, if we took the teaching of Jesus seriously as a way of life.

Love enemies	Be merciful
Do good	Judge not
Kind to the ungrateful	Condemn not
Forgive	Give

Wherever these are experienced – there is the Church and there is Jesus known and loved.

Step four: Deeper reflections

Spend some time in small groups on one or two of the following exercises.

A. Is it realistic to think that each one of us can share "the good news" with others?

B. In what practical ways can we do this?

C. How does being a Catholic affect our attitude to work and our relationships there?

D. How does being a Catholic affect our attitude to our neighbourhood, city and world?

E. Is it true that anyone who lives a life of genuine love, no matter what religion they are(n't), is touched by the Spirit of God?

Step five: How do the stories touch each other?

What light does this Gospel story throw on the cartoons?

Step six: Prayer

Decorate the table and expose the Blessed Sacrament. Sing an appropriate hymn or choose some music.

READ THE POEM
The Face of Christ

The tragic beauty of the face of Christ
shines in the face of man;
the abandoned old live on
in shabby rooms, far from inner comfort.
Outside , in the street
din and purpose, the world like a fiery animal

reined in by youth. Within
a pallid tiring heart
shuffles about it's dwelling.

Nothing, or so little, come of life's promise.
Out of broken men, despised minds
what does one make –
a roadside show, a graveyard of the heart?

The Christian God reproves
faithless ranting minds
crushing like upper and lower stones
all life between;
Christ, fowler of street and hedgerow
of cripples and the distempered old
– eyes blind as woodknots,
tongues tight as immigrants –
takes in His gospel net
all the hue and cry of existence.

Heaven, of such imperfection,
wary, ravaged, wild?

Yes. Compel them in.   *Daniel Berrigan*

PRAY THE PRAYER OF ST FRANCIS

Lord, make me an instrument of your peace;
Where there is hatred, let me sow love;
Where there is injury, pardon;
Where there is discord, union;
Where there is doubt, faith;
Where there is despair, hope;
Where there is darkness, light;
Where there is sadness, joy.
For thy mercy and truth's sake:
O Divine Master, grant that I may not so much seek
To be consoled as to console,
To be understood as to understand,
To be loved as to love,
for
It is in giving that we receive,
It is in pardoning that we are pardoned,
It is in dying that we are born to eternal life.

Bless each person individually

Name May the Lord bless you and keep you.
May his face shine upon you and be gracious to you.
May he look upon you with kindness and give you his peace.
May almighty God bless you,
the Father, the Son and the Holy Spirit.